# A Covid

July 4, 2021

Conrad LeBeau

The origin of this book began with Report 165 in March 2020. A list of home remedies was offered for research and testing purposes in an 8-page report. This booklet is the culmination of over one year of research from multiple sources. The Covid-19 virus came to the world at warp speed early in 2020. Last year, vaccines were developed at warp speed, and then without waiting for long term testing to determine if the vaccines were actually safe, were offered to the public and promoted in the media 24/7.

This first part of this booklet has substantial information that covers many of the Covid controversies of our times including the vaccines. Experimental protocols* are proposed herein to reduce the adverse effects of the vaccines and/or from direct exposure to the whole live SARS-CoV-2 virus. Help for Covid long-haulers are also provided. *FDA not approved.

Over the past 30 years I have written several books on immune based therapies including the "Immune Restoration Handbook 4th ed" that was published last year and is co-authored by Dr. Ronald Peters MD of mindbodymc.com. Dr. Peters wrote: *"The future of medicine lies in shifting some of the responsibility for healing back to the patient....regardless of your personal health issues, it is important to regain confidence in the healing power that lives naturally within you."* "

Other books I wrote  include the medicinal uses for "Hydrogen Peroxide and Ozone", "Natural Remedies for Intestinal Health", "Insomnia and Cell Phones", and "Money Creation by Wall Street Bankers." From my perspective as a researcher, I'd say that our sources of information and beliefs strongly influence our medical and health care choices. Mass media, social media, television, propaganda, and smart phones have a major influence on our health care choices.

The practice of low-cost remedies being swept under the rug is legendary, and is why it is hard to find an integrative doctor employed by corporate medicine. What have been removed from the table of treatment options are low-cost drugs, repurposed generic drugs and natural healing remedies. These include the use of organic health foods, plants, nutrition, herbs, and other non-patentable health products. Several low cost and home remedies for Covid-19 are provided.

The following are a list of topics I will cover in this booklet:

1. **Origins of Covid**. Nature-made or Man-made? Did the Wuhan Virology lab in China do gain of function research with NIH funding as reported by Newsweek magazine in 2020?

2. **What are the mutated** or variant versions of Covid-19 viruses and should we lose sleep over them? A long list of remedies and treatment options are discussed from the conventional to the unconventional.

3. **Vaccines** - the jab in the arm. Is it really safe? No, serious adverse effects are well documented in this book. Don't be misled by the slick ads from the mass media. They sound like used car salesmen. Adverse effects of mRNA and vector vaccines include death from blood clots, blood vessel bleeding, and thrombocytopenia, as reported on Voluntary Adverse Events Reporting System (VAERS) forms at the Center for Disease Control (CDC) and in several scientific articles published in 2021.

VAERS reports of deaths field with the CDC from the Covid vaccines are 10,991 as of July 9, 2021. The reports are filed by doctors and patients from Dec 14, 2020 to date, and are updated every Friday. According to Dr. Peter McCullough MD, and based on un-named sources inside the CDC, over 50,000 deaths from all 3 Covid vaccines have occurred in the United States through July 9, 2021.

4 **Colostrum - Nature's vaccine without the jab.** Colostrum provides passive immune transfer for both prevention and treatment of Covid-19 without the drama. Oral Colostrum requires no jab and has no scary side effects.

5. **What are the Pro's and Con's of lockdowns and wearing masks?** Preventing the spread vs. hypoxia (low oxygen) isolation, depression, suicides, homicides and even insanity.

6. **Why are obese people of any age** more likely to get infected and develop serious complications from Covid-19?

7. **Is there a Covid connection to HIV?** Why are persons with AIDS who are taking their HIV meds not dying or seriously infected by Covid?

8. **Why do the Chinese insist on taking stool samples** from foreign visitors and diplomats? Why probiotics may have a role in prevention and recovery from Covid?

9. **Hydrogen peroxide (H2O2)** is a remedy to safely kill SARS-Cov-2, the virus that causes Covid-19. H2O2 can be safely used outside the body, and, at a low dose that is diluted inside the body as well. It is also highly effective added to bath water to be absorbed into the skin. SARS stand for Sudden Acute Respiratory Syndrome. H2O2 is readily available at local drug stores and is an effective and safe anti-viral medication.

I know one person with the measles and another with chicken pox. Both of them added 3 quarts of 3% hydrogen peroxide solution to a bathtub full of warm water. One person soaked for 20 minutes in the tub. The other person fell asleep and was in the tub for about one hour. Within 2 days both persons reported their skin rash had dried up and they had recovered. How it works: H2O2 is absorbed into the skin and circulates through the blood vessels to find and oxidize the viruses rendering them harmless.

10. **Treatments you can do at home** - hydrogen peroxide in bath water (or taken orally in diluted small doses), fermented foods, herbs, nutritional supplements and repurposed drugs that are effective in treating Covid-19 are presented. Multiple choices are discussed with antiviral, anti-inflammatory benefits, and that may offer protection against Covid infection of blood vessel ACE2 receptors.

11. **Covid-19 long haulers** may have lingering SARS-Cov-2 virus active and shedding in the intestines, even though it is gone from the sinuses and lungs. An 8 part home protocol is proposed to speed recovery and finish eradicating the virus from the body. Bring an end to brain fog, fatigue, shortness of breath, depression, digestive distress and safely remove small blood clots caused by

the SARS-Cov-2 infection of blood vessels. Life style habits and dietary choices are discussed that will impair or help with recovery from Covid-19.

12. **Average Age of Covid Deaths**. What is the average age of people living in the United States who died from Covid-19 in 2020?. Answer - the average age was 78. In 2020, the average life span of persons living in the United States was 77.* Also, 99% of those who died at any age from Covid-19 had comorbidities.

Note: These figures were cited by Tucker Carlson in his Fox TV program on July 8, 2021.

*Data Source: city-data.com

## Anatomy of the Covid-19 Infection
## From Initial Infection to Systemic Illness

1. Most transmissions of SARS-CoV-2 are airborne with the virus being exhaled by one person and inhaled by another person within close proximity. However, if the SARS-CoV-2 infection becomes systemic and sheds in the intestines, the virus could be sexually transmitted.

2. Initial infection is in the mucosal passageways of the sinuses and lungs where the Sars-Cov virus **Spike protein** attaches itself to the ACE2 receptor to infect the blood vessels and organs. **ACE2** receptor is called the Angiotension-converting enzyme 2 that lowers and regulates blood pressure.

3. From infection of the ACE2 receptor sites, the Covid virus is carried by the blood vessels to all parts of the body including the organs, glands, and intestines. Inflammation of the blood vessels is a signature mark of Sars-Cov infections. Other markers are declines in platelet counts, easy bruising, bleeding, nerve damage, blood clots, and strokes.

4. The immune system response involves *B cells* to initiate *antibody* production, T cell activity to determine the foreign protein invader, and *neutrophil* activity. Neutrophils are a type of white blood cell that, as their first line of defense, produce *hydrogen peroxide* to kill all types of foreign viruses, fungus, parasites and germs. While antibodies provide short-term protection against infections, usually measured in months,

**Memory T cells** can provide long term protection that spans several years.

5. After the virus has been cleared from the respiratory tract, the infection can still be present in the intestines and may continue to persist in some blood vessels and other body parts causing a variety of symptoms. Hence the term - **Covid Long Haulers** - a not so small group of chronically infected persons. Total clearance of the Sars-Cov-2 virus from the intestines is necessary to end long-term symptoms. An Internet search may yield a Covid support group near you.

## Origins of Covid. Nature-made or Man-made?

### The NIH funded research on Coronavirus in bats at Wuhan Lab

The following are excerpts from Newsweek - Dec 20, 2020

"just last year, the National Institute for *Allergy and Infectious Diseases, the organization led by Dr. Fauci, funded scientists at the Wuhan Institute of Virology and other institutions for work on gain-of-function research on bat coronaviruses.*

*"In 2019, with the backing of NIAID, the National Institutes of Health committed $3.7 million over six years for research that included some gain-of-function work. The program followed another $3.7 million, 5-year project for collecting and studying bat coronaviruses, which ended in 2019, bringing the total to $7.4 million.*

*"Many scientists have criticized gain of function research, which involves manipulating viruses in the lab to explore their potential for infecting humans, because it creates a risk of starting a pandemic from accidental release.*

*"SARS-CoV-2 , the virus now causing a global pandemic, is believed to have originated in bats. U.S. intelligence, after originally asserting that the coronavirus had occurred naturally, conceded last month that the pandemic may have originated in a leak from the Wuhan lab."*

End of quote from Newsweek magazine.

The former director of the CDC, Dr. Robert Redfield, bravely told his opinion recently (May 2021) on live TV that the Covid-19 virus was made and leaked from the Wuhan Lab of Virology in China. Also, Dr. Sanjay Gupta of CNN had the backbone and good judgment to back up Dr. Redfield. Congratulations to both of them.

## Gain of Function Research funded by the Chinese Communist Party and National Institute of Health.

Dr. Li Meng Yan appeared on the Tucker Carlson Television Show on the Fox News Channel on Feb 6, 2020 and again on May 21, 2021. Dr. Yan is a Chinese virologist who worked at the Wuhan Lab in 2019 and later defected to the United States. She told Tucker Carlson that the Chinese Communist Party (CCP) financed research on the corona viruses for possible military purposes. What is baffling is why would the NIH fund research at the Wuhan Virology Lab? Are not the U.S. and the Chinese Communists at odds for other political reasons?

Gain of Function research is when virologists try to combine viruses or parts of viruses, and testing to determine how dangerous or contagious they can become in a world-wide pandemic. This type of research needs to stop. We already have more than enough other problems in this world.

In May, 2021, President Joe Biden ordered the US Intelligence Agencies to review the available data and write a report on the origins of the Coronavirus. The report is due by Aug 31 2021.

## Mutated variants of Covid-19

As millions of people in the United States and around the world get inoculated with the Pfizer, Moderna, J and J, AstraZeneca, Novavax, Sputnik and other vaccines. The emergence of variant or mutated versions of the original Covid-19 virus could render the present vaccines less effective or, not effective at all.

Mutations in viruses usually weaken over a period of time but these current mutations are reported to be more easily transmitted and create more severe illness. The UK variant of Covid-19 called B.1.1.7 is now the most active in the United States.

In a best-case scenario, the vaccines will maintain some effectiveness against the mutants. In a worse case scenario, the mutated Covid viruses may render the vaccines ineffective or, the vaccines side effects could become a greater threat to public health than the active SARS-Cov-2 virus. Here is a short list of current mutants. This list is expected to grow.

The Center for Disease Control (cdc.gov) states that there are five Variants Of Concern (VOCs) in the United States as of April 2nd 2021.

The five variants (mutated viruses) are:

**B.1.1.7**: This variant was first identified in the US in December 2020. It was initially detected in the UK.

**B.1.351**: This variant was first identified in the US at the end of January 2021. It was initially detected in South Africa in December 2020.

**P.1:** This variant was first detected in the US in January 2021. P.1 was initially identified in travelers from Brazil, who were tested during routine screening at an airport in Japan, in early January.

**B.1.427 and B.1.429**: These two variants were first identified in California in February 2021 and were classified as VOCs in March 2021. Source: cdc.gov

**The Covid Delta Variant from India**. The latest Covid variant to draw the media's attention is the Delta strain from India. This strain is supposed to infect faster and cause more serious adverse effects than the other variants. Shortly after this booklet goes to press, there will yet another variant of concern to talk about. Now, there is the Llamda variant from Peru.

What the politicians and public health officials are missing is the need to find and rapidly test safe low cost treatments for whatever new strain comes along; and this they are not doing. Fauci and the NIH now say they are working on a pill to treat the Covid-19 infection. If Fauci and the drug companies invent a new pill to treat Covid, it will be patented, expensive, and the NIH will probably get a cut in the sales - a conflict of interest.

Today, there are more than a dozen low cost treatments available for Covid-19 that are safe, effective, and low cost. A few require a doctor's prescription but most are readily available over-the-counter (OTC) to the informed person.

# Covid19 found in Fecal Matter

Intestinal Incubation preceded Pneumonia - Key findings of the American Gastroenterology… Assn. (2)

- Significant numbers of coronavirus patients have diarrhea, nausea, and vomiting and/or abdominal discomfort before developing respiratory symptoms.
- Researchers recommend monitoring patients with initial GI distress, which will allow for earlier detection, diagnosis, isolation and intervention.
- Viral RNA is detectable in stool of patients with suspected coronavirus; it is now clear that the virus sheds into the stool.
- Viral gastrointestinal infection and potential fecal-oral transmission can last even after viral clearance in respiratory tract.
- Prevention of fecal-oral transmission should be taken into consideration to control the spread the virus.

Ref:
1. GI symptoms and potential fecal transmission in coronavirus patients.
https://medicalxpress.com/news/2020-03-gi-symptoms-potential-fecal-transmission.html
2. Nature Medicine - Characteristics of pediatric SARS-CoV-2 infection and potential evidence for persistent fecal viral shedding.

Editor's Note: if the coronavirus can be eliminated in the intestines, respiratory failure and pneumonia might also be preventable. It is my theory that some Covid long haulers who survive the pneumonia part of the Covid-19 infection cycle also have a persistent infection of the virus in their intestines and because of that have symptoms including fatigue, shortness of breath with physical exertion, brain fog, and mental depression.

To get rid of the intestinal infection and lingering symptoms will require a substantial change in lifestyle and diet. There is no vaccine or simple pill from any source that will quickly fix that problem just like there is no FDA approved drug guaranteed to cure any disease including Covid-19.

## Gut Symptoms in Covid19

In addition to the symptoms seen in children, adults may also have lethargy, dyspnea, muscle ache, headache, nausea, diarrhea, vomiting, stomach cramps and disorientation. Nasal swabs are not enough to clear a person for covid19 as this study from China has found covid19 in fecal swabs indicating that a possible intestinal infection may continue even after the nasal swabs find no more viruses. (1,2)

Significant numbers of coronavirus patients have diarrhea, nausea, and vomiting and/or abdominal discomfort before developing respiratory symptoms.

Researchers recommend monitoring patients with initial GI distress, which will allow for earlier detection, diagnosis, isolation and intervention. Viral RNA is detectable in stool of patients with suspected coronavirus; it is now clear that the virus sheds into the stool.

Viral gastrointestinal infection and potential fecal-oral transmission can last even after viral clearance in respiratory tract. Prevention of fecal-oral transmission should be taken into consideration to control the spread the virus.

Ref:

1. GI symptoms and potential fecal transmission in coronavirus patients. https://medicalxpress.com/news/2020-03-gi-symptoms-potential-fecal-transmission.html

2. Nature Medicine - Characteristics of pediatric SARS-CoV-2 infection and potential evidence for persistent fecal viral shedding.

## China requires all new diplomats to provide rectal swab samples for Covid-19 before entry

WOW! You are not likely to see a drive through line for this test. The Chinese know what is already published in the scientific literature, that you can test negative with a nasal swab and still have the Covid-19 virus in your intestines.

On March 3 2021, the New York Post quoting the UK Times reported that -

*"China has made anal COVID-19 swabs mandatory for all foreign travelers arriving in the country, a report said Wednesday. The government has claimed that such tests provide a higher degree of accuracy than other screening methods for the virus,....*

*"As part of the new travel requirement, there will be testing hubs in Beijing and Shanghai airports, the outlet reported. Li Tongzeng, a respiratory disease medic, said the anal swabs are better because virus traces stay in fecal samples longer than they do in the nose or throat, state media reported."*

## Ivermectin and Hydroxychloroquine (quinine)

What they won't tell you is that it is completely unnecessary to develop a new drug to treat Covid as several low cost treatment are already available. One combination includes the use of both **Ivermectin** and **Hydrochloroquine**. These two repurposed drugs are already FDA approved and have had more than half a century of history behind their safe use.

Ivermectin has broad antiviral properties and HCQ is a well known anti-inflammatory, an antimalarial drug that is a synthetic version of quinine. Today, the Delta strain is being successfully treated in some provinces in India with a combination of these two drugs. The western media has parroted a disinformation campaign against these two worthy drugs and many other low cost remedies for Covid-19. Completely ignored or shunned are the use of **low dose hydrogen peroxide**, **thymol** from thyme and oregano, **grapefruit seed extract** and **wormwood**, **raw garlic**, **cayenne**, and **colostrum**.

## Why Statements and Opinions from Regulatory Agencies cannot always be trusted

While throughout history, vaccinations generally have saved more lives than they have lost, there are exceptions to this general statement. Today, there are both media and government cover-ups of current adverse effects of Covid vaccines and some other vaccines as well.  These cover-ups are intentional and there is a long history of them.

First, the Hepatitis B Vaccine (HBV) was distributed to the gay community in the United States in the 1980s and, unknown to the recipients, this vaccine was contaminated with live HIV virus. The following is an excerpt from Positive Health News #10 in 1996: (1)

*"Late in 1980, the first cases of GRID (Gay Related Immune Deficiency) appeared in New York City. At about the same time, Haiti had an outbreak of both African Swine Fever and AIDS (2). The Hepatitis B vaccination trials were in progress in the gay community. When an (HIV) infected donor's blood was used in the development of*

*the Hepatitis B vaccine, this quickly spread the disease through major gay centers in the United States"* (*)

At about the same time, the WHO distributed vaccines in Africa that were also contaminated with live HIV and millions of Africans were infected. There were reports (not all sourced here) at the time that the U.S government was involved in gain of function research with the African Swine Fever (ASF) virus at Ft Detrick in New Jersey. The ASF was combined with the HIV virus imported from Africa and then infected into Castro's swine population. Fidel Castro publicly blamed the CIA for germ warfare and he ordered the killing of 500,000 pigs to stop the ASF pandemic.

Haitians working in Cuba at the time were infected with either ASF or HIV or both and returned to Haiti, which became the focal point of the worldwide AIDS pandemic. Letters linking AIDS to ASFV also appeared in The Lancet (June 11, 1983) by St. John RK and a letter by Jane Teas in Ann NY Acad. Sci, 1984;437:270-2. Another on "African Swine Fever and AIDS" in The Lancet, on Mar 8, 1986 by Beldekas and Teas.

The conclusion of this trail of information is that the origin of HIV as the start of the worldwide AIDS epidemic was not an accident of nature from Africa but was the result of gain of function research paid for by the U.S. government and done at Ft. Detrick, N.J.

*Positive Health News, Jan 14, 1996 from archived articles.

## African Globe reported contaminated Tetanus vaccines laced with sterilizing agents

A website Africanglobe.net (*) reported on Nov 16, 2014 that Kenyan doctors found **HCG antigen**, a known sterilizing agent in the tetanus vaccine being given for free by WHO. Upon receiving that news, the Catholic Church in Kenya advised Kenyan women not to accept the vaccine:

*"Two UN organizations, the WHO and UNICEF, have just been caught red-handed administering "tetanus vaccines" laced with sterilizing agents to girls and women in Kenya. And as you will see below, this is not the first time that this has happened. Apparently*

Gullain Barr Syndrome (GBS)- The CDC reported in their website on vaccine safety concerning the following: (*)

*"In 1976, there was a small increased risk of GBS after swine flu vaccination, which was a special flu vaccine for a potential pandemic strain of flu virus. The National Academy of Medicine, formerly known as Institute of Medicine, conducted a scientific review of this issue in 2003 and found that people who received the 1976 swine flu vaccine had an increased risk for developing GBS. The increased risk was approximately one additional case of GBS for every 100,000 people who got the swine flu vaccine. Scientists have several theories about the cause, but the exact reason for this link remains unknown." (*)*
* www.cdc.gov/vaccinesafety/concerns/guillain-barre-syndrome.html

In the early 1990's two readers out of 2000 subscribers to the quarterly newsletter from Keep Hope Alive reported that they had developed Gullain Barr Syndrome (GBS) after receiving the Swine Flu vaccine in 1976. That is one per 1000, not one per 100,000. If you extrapolate this number, it would be 100 cases of GBS per 100,000 people or 100 times more than the NIH and CDC has admitted. The FDA and the NIH have had a bad habit of ignoring or under reporting adverse effects. This constitutes a cover-up.

While vaccinations for Covid-19 have been made widely available and nearly 200 million Americans have had one or two shots, controversy over their side effects remains as reports of blood clots, vascular inflammation, and deaths from heart attacks continues to grow.

Excessive vaccinations of all types have been liked to an increase in auto-immune diseases, outbreaks of herpes and shingles, and even dementia in the elderly. A handout sheet I read given to a vaccine recipient at the time of the Covid vaccinations did not include instructions on where or how to file an adverse vaccine event at the CDC using a VAERS report form. This must have been done deliberately to reduce adverse events from being reported to the CDC.

I listened to one man who was recently asked by a TV reporter why he did not get his second Pfizer Covid-19 shot. He said he still had a headache from the first shot and did not want to take a chance it would get worse with the second shot. The constant headache could be caused by a small blood clot in his brain, or by blood vessel inflammation caused by the spike protein attaching to ACE2 receptors in the blood vessels. Without a CT scan, there is no way of knowing what is causing his headache.

## Moderna Covid Vaccines and Thrombocytopenia (*)
## Three cases discussed and one death reported

*"Immune thrombocytopenia is a condition that causes your platelet count to fall. It causes the body's immune system to attack and destroy its own platelets and restricts the production of platelets. Bruising for no apparent reason and bleeding are common symptoms of this condition. You may experience nosebleeds, bleeding from the mouth and heavier than normal periods......*

*"One woman who reported this condition after getting the COVID-19 vaccine shot exhibited bruises on her arms and legs and bleeding blisters in her mouth a day after her first dose of Moderna's COVID vaccine in January. Another woman from Texas reported heavy vaginal bleeding and red spots on wrists and ankles. Both were successfully treated. But a 56-year-old obstetrician, who developed this condition three days after receiving the Pfizer-BioNTech vaccine in January, died of brain hemorrhage."* *

* www.thehealthsite.com by Jahnavi Sarma Feb 11, 2021

## Oxford- AstraZeneca adenovirus for SARS-CoV-2 thrombosis and thrombocytopenia with one death
published in the Journal of Neurol Neurosurg Psychiatry on May 25, 2021
Authors: Al-Mayhani T, Sabet S, Stubbs MJ, et al.

The following excerpts were downloaded from the British Medical Journal at http://jnnp.bmj.com on May 27, 2021

No 1 *"Patient 1, a 35-year-old Asian woman, developed episodic right temporal and periorbital headache 6 days after receiving the ChAdOx1 nCoV-19 vaccine. Five days later, she awoke with left face, arm and leg weakness, right gaze preference and drowsiness. Non-contrast CT and CT angiography (CTA) revealed occlu- sion of the right middle cerebral artery (MCA) distal M1 segment with extensive ischaemia and haemorrhagic transforma- tion......   "Fourteen days after presen- tation, her conscious level suddenly dropped; CT head showed extensive haemorrhagic transformation of the left MCA infarct with mass effect and herni- ation of the brain through the decompres- sive hemicraniectomy. Brainstem death was subsequently confirmed."*

No 2. *"Patient 2, a 37-year-old White female, presented 12 days after receiving the ChAdOx1 nCoV-19 vaccine with diffuse headache, left visual field loss, confu- sion and left arm weakness. CTA showed occlusion of both internal carotid arteries (figure 1E) and left transverse sinus throm- bosis (figure 1F); diffusion-weighted MRI showed bilateral acute infarcts in a borderzone distribution."*

No 3. *"Patient 3, a 43-year-old Asian male, presented 21 days after the ChAdOx1 nCoV-19 vaccine with dysphasia. CT and magnetic resonance (MR) showed an acute left frontal and insular infarct corre- sponding to the anterior cortical territory of the left MCA, with a small volume of haemorrhagic transformation within the infarct."*

The authors concluded their report stating that in addition to **venous thrombosis**, the spectrum of symptoms can also include **arterial occlusion**, **strokes**, sudden drops in **platelet counts due to antibodies** directed by the immune system at platelets infected with the spike proteins from the vaccine.  For treatments, they suggested iv immune globulin, prednisolone, plasma-pheresis and non-heparin anticoagulants.

End of article

Comment: Had the three persons in this report known of the potential of getting a stroke, blood clot or thrombocytopenia (low platelet counts), from the Covid-19 vaccine, they could have avoided this and the one death by not getting the vaccine in the first place. The article includes 8 x-ray photographs. It is apparent that these vaccines are not safe and should be stopped.

### 5 REFERENCES of Covid Vaccine Adverse Effects in 2021

J Neurol Neurosurg Psychiatry Month 2021 Vol 0 No 0
1 Scully M, Singh D, Lown R, et al. Pathologic antibodies to platelet factor 4 after ChAdOx1 nCoV-19 vaccination. N Engl J Med 2021. 04 16, 2021].
2. Greinacher A, Thiele T, Warkentin TE, et al. Thrombotic thrombocytopenia after ChAdOx1 nCov-19 vaccination. N Engl J Med 2021. Apr 9, 2021].
3. Schultz NH, Sørvoll IH, Michelsen AE, et al. Thrombosis and thrombocytopenia after

ChAdOx1 nCoV-19 vaccination. N Engl J Med 2021. Apr 9 2021].
4. Cines DB, Bussel JB. SARS-CoV-2 vaccine-induced immune thrombotic thrombocytopenia. N Engl J Med 2021. 16 Apr 2021].
5. Oldenburg J, Klamroth R, Langer F, et al. Diagnosisand management of vaccine-related thrombosis following AstraZeneca COVID-19 vaccination: guidance statement from the GTH. Hamostaseologie 2021. 01 Apr 2021].

## Jeff O, a local 59 y.o. Maintenance man dies a few days after receiving the J & J Covid-19 vaccine

Conrad LeBeau 5/8/21
Jeff had previously rented an apt from me in Milwaukee, WI. On Palm Sunday, March 28th he called me and asked for a ride to UMOS, (a local Community Health center) to get a Covid-19 vaccine shot. I was unable to give him a ride that day because of a scheduling conflict.

On April 26th, his uncle, called to tell me that Jeff had passed away on April 22. I contacted his daughter who told me the last time she spoke to her dad was Sunday April 18th. I learned that Jeff told her he was not feeling well and blamed the J and J Covid vaccine that he had received the previous week at the UMOS Community Health Center.

On May 5th, convinced that Jeff did not die from Emphysema since he could walk half a mile without his oxygen tank, I filed a VAERS report with the CDC online. [The family asked me not to publish their names and phone numbers as they wanted their privacy.]

## Sara Stickles - a 28-year-old woman from Beloit WI, dies 5 days after 2nd Pfizer Vaccine

Feb 2021. Within 5 days of vaccination, Sara Stickles (*) suffered fatal side effects from the Covid-19 vaccine. Sara Stickles was the mother of a little boy, and was a healthcare worker at the Swedish American Hospital. She suffered a brain aneurysm and is now brain dead just 5 days after receiving the second experimental mRNA COVID injection from Pfizer.

The sister of the vaccine victim, Jacqueline F. Gifford, monitored the rapid deterioration in Stickles health and shared the changes on Facebook. According to the family, immediately after the vaccine shot, a rash began to appear all over the body. For the next 5 days, Stickles suffered migraines. Before hospitalization, she lost the ability to speak, her eyes crossed and glazed over, before she lost consciousness, wrote Gifford.

*(Source: lifesitenews.com and other internet sources)

## New York Times reports on a bleeding disorder linked to Moderna's Covid vaccine

Published Feb. 8, 2021 Updated Feb. 10, 2021

Author Denise Grady states:

*"One day after receiving her first dose of Moderna's Covid vaccine, Luz Legaspi, 72, woke up with bruises on her arms and legs, and blisters that bled inside her mouth. She was hospitalized in New York City that day, Jan. 19, with a severe case of immune thrombocytopenia — a lack of platelets, a blood component essential for clotting.*

*"The same condition led to the death in January of Dr. Gregory Michael, 56, an obstetrician in Miami Beach whose symptoms appeared three days after he received the Pfizer-BioNTech vaccine. Treatments failed to restore his platelets, and after two weeks in the hospital he died from a brain hemorrhage."*

## From Practical Cardiology published June 18 2021
## Case Series Details Treatment of Myocarditis-Like Illness Following COVID-19 Vaccination

by Patrick Campbell

The following are excerpts -

*"A case series of 7 patients from a pair of US medical centers details the treatment and presentation of patients with myocarditis-like illness after receiving a COVID-19 vaccine. The American Heart Association is calling attention to a new study detailing the treatment of temporary myocarditis among patients who received a COVID-19 vaccine.*

*"With perimyocarditis reported as a rare vaccination complication, the study reports a case series of 7 patients hospitalized with acute myocarditis-like illness following vaccination and provides insight into treatment of these patients, all of whom had symptoms resolve and were discharged within 4 days of admission......"*

The 7 cases were published in the magazine "Circulation," and describe seven male patients treated at 2 medical centers in Virginia and Texas.

## June 13, 2021 - Questions I submitted to Pfizermedicalinformation.com

Conrad LeBeau in an email to Pfizer:

There is substantial published research (at PubMed) that the spike protein on the live Covid-19 virus attaches to and infects the ACE2 receptor lining blood vessels, platelets and some organs. The Pfizer website makes no mention of whether or not the spike protein from the Covid-19 virus in their vaccine attaches itself to the ACE2 receptor sites in the blood vessels, platelets or organs. Pfizer makes no mention of whether or not their vaccine contains actual bioactive (live) spike proteins.

This is really an important issue because if the vaccine only contained harmless, inert or inactivated particles of the covid-19 virus then it could not possibly be causing all these inflammatory effects including bleeding, inflammation of the lining of the blood vessels, blood clots, heart attacks, strokes and death. Only a live virus or a live piece of the Covid-19 virus would be capable of causing all these inflammatory reactions.

Since Pfizer is totally silent on the question of whether or not their vaccine contains living spike proteins and there are over 5888 reports of deaths (June 4 2021) from the Pfizer, Moderna and J and J vaccines linked in VAERS reports filed with the CDC, the spike virus in the Pfizer and Moderna vaccines must be much alive.

**First Question**: what specific type of white blood cells (examples are macrophages, neutrophils, T cells, cd4 cells, cd8 cells and others) would produce copies of the spike protein in the Pfizer Covid 19 vaccine?

**Second Question**: Do the spike proteins produced by the immune cells as a result of the injected Pfizer Covid vaccine also attach themselves to ACE2 receptors lining blood vessels and organs in the body?

**Third Question**: Does the antibody response and or the T cell response destroy those spike proteins that are attached to the ACE2 receptors lining the blood vessels?

**Fourth Question**: Has Pfizer found that the immune response of the B cells and T cells that destroy the spike proteins attached to the ACE2 receptors on the blood vessels also damages the blood vessel walls, destroy platelets, or form blood clots or cause blood vessel leakage?

Please reply ASAP. July 12 2021 - no response from Pfizer yet. Pfizer's response will be inserted here if I get a reply before this booklet is published. After searching Pfizer entire website, not one word about ACE2 receptors could be found and not one word was mentioned by Pfizer about inflammation of the lining of the heart, or that blood clots and circulatory disease could impact some people negatively after the Pfizer shots.

The Pfizer and Moderna vaccines both use the mRNA technology for developing their vaccines. An elderly lady friend of my older brother got both of the Moderna shots in April and 3 weeks after the second shot, she vomited blood profusely on May 16th. She was rushed to the hospital and is recovering following several blood transfusions. Her platelet count was low and may have been a factor in the bleeding.

It is possible the Moderna shots caused her platelet counts to drop after she received the second shot from an autoimmune reaction. This could occur when a subset of white blood cells would attack the platelet cells infected with the spike proteins from the Moderna vaccine. Why hasn't the FDA and the NIH insisted on a controlled study to measure declines in the platelet counts following jabs from the Pfizer, Moderna or J and J vaccines?

## April 17, 2021 India's Health Ambassador Vivek Dies One Day after taking the Covid Vaccine

Popular Tamil actor and comedian Vivekh died this morning in the hospital hours after he was admitted for cardiac arrest. The 59-year-old was in critical condition in a Chennai hospital after a cardiac arrest on Thursday morning. He was brought in unconscious at 11 am, was resuscitated, and subsequently underwent coronary angiogram and then angioplasty.

Medical bulletin said he was critical on ECMO support, which pumps and oxygenates blood outside the body, but died at 4:35 am today. On Thursday, the actor was declared as state's ambassador for creating public health messages o promote vaccination. He took the COVID-19 vaccine Covaxin in Tamil Nadu Hospital in Chennai and urged others to take the vaccine.

His vaccination was at a public event with TV channels carrying photographs of him taking the shot. As the cardiac arrest happened less than 24 hours after the inoculation, there were questions raised whether he died due to the side effects of the vaccine.

## Children's Health Defense.org*

May 4, 2021. (reprinted by Childrenshealthdefense.org)
Last week, Center for Food Safety** filed a Freedom of Information Act (FOIA) lawsuit against the National Institutes of Health (NIH), an agency with the U.S. Department of Health and Human Services (HHS). Center for Food Safety is suing the agency over its failure to release government documents related to the approval and issuance of NIH contracts and grants that fund research projects involving controversial gain of function/gain of threat studies with dangerous, so-called "enhanced potential pandemic pathogens."

*"The NIH's refusal to make public the research it is funding to enhance the transmissibility, infectiousness and lethality of potential pandemic viruses is grossly irresponsible,"* said Andrew Kimbrell, executive director of Center for Food Safety.**

*"We are litigating to get that information because transparency and public knowledge about these highly hazardous experiments could be an important step in avoiding the next pandemic."*

* childrenshealthdefense.org - Chairman Robert Kennedy Jr.
** centerforfoodsafety.org

## US Covid Vaccine deaths CDC's Voluntary Adverse Events Reporting System (VAERS) database

VAERS is the CDC website stats on adverse events and

fatalities voluntarily reported to the CDC by doctors and patients who received vaccines. The VAERS site has a form for reporting adverse events from any vaccine including the Covid vaccines. The site also has links with training instructions on how to access all the data. They don't make it easy for the public to file a report of an adverse event or to search the database of reports filed by the public or doctors.

When I filed a VAERS report with the CDC about a friend's death from the J and J vaccine, the CDC website popup calendar failed to insert the date of death I selected. I had to type in the date of his death in another part of the form. This might explain why CHD reported that the VAERS link at the CDC listed over 300 deaths with no date of death listed. That is what happens when the CDC's website link for the VAERS online form malfunctions. I question whether this computer malfunction was really accidental.

Go to https://vaers.hhs.gov/index.html Note: if this link is blocked, go to cdc.gov and type in the word VAERS in the search box to reach the data base site and online links to file a report of side effects from a vaccine or to read training instructions on how to search the CDC database.

CNN (that pushes the vaccine day and night), Pizer, Moderna and J and J must have something to hide or they would contact the CDC for the names of medical doctors who filed these VAERS reports and interview them. It is also true that these drug companies had laws passed so they cannot be sued for damages.

An elderly lady interviewed by Tucker Carlson on June 16, 2021 stated her husband who got the Covid shot has 100 blood clots in his lungs and her son, an athlete, has two blood clots in his brain from the Covid shots.

**Editors Note: Openvaers.com/covid-data** reports (2) the COVID Vaccine Data is 358,379 adverse reports through June 11, 2021 and 5,993 vaccine related deaths. Studies cited by Children's Health Defense indicate that (1 to 13%) of all adverse events following a vaccination are reported to the CDC VAERS website. Thus, Covid vaccine deaths reported on VAERS represent about 1/7th of the total deaths caused by the mRNA and vector vaccines. (2) https://www.openvaers.com/covid-data

# July 2, 2021 Updated CDC Vaccine deaths - 9048

From childrenshealthdefense.org by Megan Redshaw

"*Data released today by the Centers for Disease Control and Prevention (CDC) included 9,048 reports of deaths, across all age groups, following COVID vaccines — an increase of more than 2,000 compared with the previous week. The data comes directly from reports submitted to the Vaccine Adverse Event Reporting System (VAERS).*

"*VAERS is the primary government-funded system for reporting adverse vaccine reactions in the U.S. Reports submitted to VAERS require further investigation before a causal relationship can be confirmed.*

"*Every Friday, VAERS makes public all vaccine injury reports received as of a specified date, usually about a week prior to the release date.*

"*Data released today show that between Dec. 14, 2020 and July 2, 2021, a total of 438,441 total adverse events were reported to VAERS, including 9,048 deaths — an increase of 2,063 over the previous week. There were 41,015 serious injury reported during the same time period — up 6,950 compared with last week.*"

## June 25 2021. Dr. Peter McCullough states that whistleblowers inside the CDC claim that the Covid injections have already killed 50,000 Americans. (1)

"*Dr Peter McCullough is professor of medicine and vice chief of internal medicine at Baylor University and also teaches at Texas A&M University. He is an epidemiologist, cardiologist and internist and has testified before the Texas State Senate related to COVID-19 treatments. He holds the distinction of being the most widely cited physician in the treatment of COVID-19 with citations in the National Library of Medicine.*" (1)

Dr McCullough states: "*We have now a whistleblower inside the CMS, and we have two whistleblowers in the CDC. We think we have 50,000 dead Americans. Fifty thousand deaths. So we actually have more deaths due to the vaccine per day than certainly the viral illness by far. It's basically propagandized bioterrorism by injection.*

*He said the suppression of early COVID treatments, such as* **hydroxychloroquine** *and especially* **Ivermectin** *"was tightly* *linked to the development of a vaccine. Without the suppression of the already-available treatments, the government would not have been able to legally grant Emergency Use Authorization to the three vaccines rushed to market by Moderna, Pfizer and Johnson and Johnson. In the case of Moderna, the U.S. government is co-patent holder through the National Institutes of Health, a clear conflict of interest."*

*"I published basically the only two papers that teach doctors how to treat COVID-19 at home to prevent hospitalization and death…If treated early, it results in an 85 percent reduction in hospitalizations and death," McCullough said.*

*"So not only were the vaccines rolled out unnecessarily by suppressing already available, effective treatments, but the FDA and CDC are now covering up tragic numbers of deaths caused by their experimental mRNA injections."*

Unless the following link is blocked by search engines like Google, you can read more of Dr. McCullough's statements here.
(1) leohohmann.com/2021/06/21/behind-the-vaccine-veil-doctor-cites-whistleblowers-inside-cdc-who-claim-injections-have-already-killed-50000-americans/

## Why the Covid-19 vaccines containing live "Spike Proteins" are alive and dangerous

For the Sars-Cov-2 virus, the spike protein is the most dangerous part of this coronavirus. The spike protein attaches to ACE2 receptors that are widely disseminated in blood vessels, platelets, various glands and organs. It then takes over and makes the infected cells produce more Sars-Cov-2 viruses. Now, with the inflammation created by the viral infection: the white blood cells respond to fight the infection and blood clots form, platelet counts decline, and bruising and bleeding sets in. The vaccines have now demonstrated an ability to cause hundreds of small blood clots in the lungs and elsewhere in the body.

In designing the vaccines, Pfizer, Moderna and Johnson and Johnson picked the most damaging part of the Sars-Cove 2 virus to duplicate - the spike protein. If inactivated spike proteins were first killed by oxidation, UV light, flash pasteurization or silver nitrate in the vaccine, the problem of vaccines causing blood clots, strokes, aneurysms or heart inflammation would stop. The estimates of 50,000 deaths from the Covid vaccines for the first 6 months of 2021 can be calculated as about 1 in 3000 persons from the general population who are fully vaccinated during the first half of 2021. Anyone want to join that lottery- it's free!

## An analogy - comparing Covid-19 to a swords tip

Think of it this way. You have a sword called Covid-19 and it is a virus you can catch by breathing air and you decide to create a vaccine to protect people against it by clipping off the tip of this sword, and create a vaccine and instruct the immune system to make thousands of copies of these sword tips to circulate all through the body. The sword's tip is the Spike protein. The promoters, say it is harmless as it is only contains the RNA. It is suppose to trigger a massive immune response and make millions of antibodies to protect you from the real virus. What could possibly go wrong with this arrangement?

1. For this approach to work, you need healthy people with robust immune systems to receive and quickly react to this mRNA vaccine. The response to this vaccine must be quick to stop the sword tips (Spike protein) from attaching to the blood vessels and doing irreparable damage and causing the same cardiovascular problems as the whole sword (SARS-CoV-2) virus that also attaches to the ACE2 blood vessel site.

2. If the person who receives the vaccine is obese, he may have an immune system that is tired, stressed out from using too many drugs, too many vaccines, too much sugar, and junk foods, herbicides in wheat, corn, and soy, environmental chemicals, antibiotics, hormones in meat, and electromagnetic pollution.  The person so inoculated may die from the same complications of the vaccine as if the real whole SARs-Cov-2 virus had been injected.

To put this in a few words, because the spike protein is very much alive and thousands of copies are being replicated by cells with the ACE2 receptor, the massive influx of spike proteins from the vaccine may kill or permanently injure the patient before his plasma derived B cells produce enough antibodies to neutralize the infection. Described this way- the Covid jab might cause you to bleed to death, cause hundreds of blood clots to form in your lungs and brain, and you may die from a heart attack or stroke.

# Suggestions on how to neutralize the Covid vaccine

First, you must treat the Pfizer and Moderna mRNA and Johnson and Johnson vector vaccines the same as if you were just inoculated with the whole live Sars-Cov-2 virus that has caused this worldwide pandemic. You may not have time to dither around and wait to see if you are going to have any adverse reactions.

Many people don't think for themselves and listen to the voice of authority (usually their TV set or Smartphone). It is time for more people to wake up and question the voice of government authority and the mass media. If you want good advice for any purpose in your life, turn to God and pray. God will not let you down or mislead you. God does need the advertising dollars from TV promotional ads. To neutralize the vaccine, let me describe several methods.

## The Hydrogen Peroxide in bathwater method

The day you plan to get the Covid jab, add 3 quarts of 3% hydrogen peroxide to a tub full of hot water and take a 20-minute bath. Do this about one hour before you are scheduled to get the jab.  If hydrogen peroxide is not available, add 1 cup of full strength choline bleach to the bath water. Hydrogen peroxide is preferred as this is what neutrophils (a special type of White Blood cell) create and use against all types of pathogens as a first line of defense.

If you get the Covid jab before you took the 20 minute bath with the 3 quarts of hydrogen peroxide added, then you must take this bath as soon as possible after you get home to reduce or prevent life any threatening adverse affects from the vaccine.

## No Bathtub? An Alternative to the bath method

Add 7 drops of 35% Hydrogen Peroxide to a full glass of water and drink this very 2 hours for up to 6 times a day times a day on the day of the inoculation. Repeat this oral $H2O2$ treatment one more day after the day of the jab. If food grade 35% is not available, then use regular 3% $H2O2$ from the drug store and increase the dose to 1 teaspoon mixed in a glass of water and take it every to 2 hours apart the day of, and the day after the jab. Food grade H2O2 is sold in some health food stores and drug stores. Do not buy or store it in a refrigerator or in a clear bottle. Store H2O2 only in a brown bottle for safety reasons.

**Note**: I do agree with the following medical advice from the two comedians - Stephen Colbert and Ellen DeGeneres- Do not drink a glass or bottle of any full strength bleach, as it will kill you. Also, the Comedians forgot to mention that you should not take a whole bottle any prescription drugs and swallow them all at once either or that will also kill you.

## The Benefits of Colostrum - Mothers' first milk

Colostrum is the first milk secreted from the mammary glands of mammals (cows, sheep, goats, buffalo, swine, dogs, cats etc.) and also humans after birth of their offspring. Colostrum is a lipid rich source of food, probiotics and multiple immune factors to immunize the new born against viruses, germ, parasites and other pathogens. Colostrum is produced mainly in the first two days of milk secretions.

Bovine Colostrum (from cows) is the first milk the suckling calf receives. It has a slightly sweet yellowish color due to its high fat content. It is rich in antibodies (immunoglobulins), particularly IgA. It has growth factors, lactoferrin, antibacterial peptides and nutrients. It supplies the calf with passive immunity before its own active immune system is established. When a mammal such as a cow is injected with a foreign virus, an immune reaction that includes a fever. The resulting antibodies and other immune factors are produced and will circulate in the blood of the animal and end up in the milk. All the immune factors are especially concentrated in the first milk of a newborn called Colostrum.

Mammals are not the only living species that can transfer immune factors to their offspring, so can chickens. When a chicken is inoculated with a virus, the immune factors end up in the eggs. To pass on the immunity in Colostrum or immunized eggs, they would need to be consumed in a raw state. If pasteurized or cooked, many of the immune factors in either Colostrum or immunized eggs will be damaged or destroyed.

A study using Colostrum was done to investigate whether Colostrum given orally can influence the severe diarrhea associated with HIV infection. A Colostrum based product called ColoPlus was used in the Nigerian study with 30 participants. The Colostrum based product called ColoPlus inhibited diarrhea, reduced fatigue, increased body weight and CD4 counts.

## ColoPlus, a new product based on Bovine Colostrum alleviated HIV-associated diarrhea.

Authors-  Florén CH, Chinenye S, Elfstrand L, Hagman C, Ihse I. by Scand J Gastroenterol. 2006 Jun;41(6):682-6.

The following are excerpts from the Scandinavian Journal of Gastroenterology:

*"Bovine Colostrum is the first milk the suckling calf receives from the cow. It is rich in immunoglobulins, growth factors, antibacterial peptides and nutrients. It supplies the calf with a passive immunity before its own active immunity is established. ColoPlus is a product based on bovine Colostrum and is designed for slow passage through the gastrointestinal tract, as well as having a high nutritional value. The aim of the study was to investigate whether ColoPlus given orally can influence the severe diarrhea associated with HIV infection."*

*"MATERIAL AND METHODS: The study was carried out at Braithwaite Memorial Specialist Hospital, Port Harcourt, Nigeria. The effects on the frequency of stool evacuations per day, on body-weight, fatigue, hemoglobin levels and CD4+ counts before (week 1) and after treatment with ColoPlus (week 7) were measured. "*

*"RESULTS: There was a dramatic decrease in stool evacuations per day from 7.0+/-2.7 to 1.3+/-0.5 (+/-SD), a substantial decrease in self-estimated fatigue of 81%, an increase in body-weight of 7.3 kg per patient and an increase in CD4+ count by 125%.*

The authors concluded that ColoPlus was an important immune based treatment for HIV-associated diarrhea.

# Scientific Research and Articles on Colostrum

The Sovereign Health Initiative (SHI) website has links to over 44 scientific articles on the health, healing and immunotherapy benefits of Colostrum for an amazing range of health conditions. Example: One study cited by SHI found that Colostrum was more effective than vaccines in preventing and shortening the duration of the seasonal flu. In addition researchers have found the following benefits of using bovine colostrum:

1. Safe and Effective for treating Clostridium Difficile.
2. Increased cytotoxicity of Natural Killer Cells - anti-cancer.
3. HIV - stops diarrhea, increases weight and CD4s.
4. Seasonal flu - more effective than vaccines in prevention.
5. Effective against e-coli and rotavirus.
6. Protects against damage to the intestinal mucosa.
7. Helps repair damage to the intestines caused by NSAIDS.
8. Colostrum's lactoferrin lyses breast and colon tumor cells.
9. Increased maturation and function of B and T, and NK cells.
10. Colostrum improved upper body strength, muscle thickness.
11. Colostrum increases lean body mass and lung function.
12. Colostrum improves cognitive function.
13. IGF-1 in Colostrum protects nerve cells.
14. Promotes the healing of tendons and ligaments.

Links to scientific articles and expert opinion are provided at
http://www.sovereignhealthinitiative.org/research/ref_health.html

Colostrum is a mother's first milk for her infant - it is nature's vaccine without the drama (fetal cells, sterilization additives to make couples childless, and questionable preservatives). Colostrum is a product of nature, has immune factors like lactoferrin immunoglobulin's that are effective for most types of infectious diseases.

On June 15 2020, the FDA sent a warning letter to Sovereign Health to cease making claims that their Vitamin C product and their Colostrum products may help mitigate the effects of Covid - 19. In order to stay in business, Sovereign withdrew the language to which that the FDA objected. The FDA dissed the following:

Under the heading "Coronavirus Precautions: Best Practices for Preventing Wuhan Coronavirus Infection": "Don't Forget Mother's

Nature's Original Vaccine …Long before … vaccines, colostrum from ruminant animals … was a primary source of both nutrition and immunity." The blog then lists lactoferrin as one of the "anti-microbial nutrients" in colostrum and asserts that "Lactoferrin … kills bacteria, viruses, and fungi."

## FDA's ignores Science in its Warning Letter on Colostrum and Vitamin C

Since the FDAs word on any topic is often treated as some kind of unimpeachable dogma, I decided to check the National Library of Medicine to see how much attention to science the FDA listens to before composing these warning letters. A search at PubMed at the NLM using the word lactoferrin yielded links to 9,026 scientific articles. When these two words are paired together (lactoferrin) and (Covid) the result is 41 published studies. None of these published studies I have read supports the FDA opinion to not use of lactoferrin.

Many authors suggested that Lactoferrin be tested as an adjunct treatment for Covid-19. From the NIH and FDA, not one word of support or interest in even a small controlled test study for using lactoferrin to shorten or diminish the duration of a Covid-19 infection. While hundreds of thousands of people die during the pandemic, the FDA and the NIH prefer to follow the money trail to the big drug companies and not to low cost remedies that are already available. The NIH and the FDA ignore the science for using herbal, dietary and repurposed drugs like Ivermectin and Quinine. Where are the public disclosures of conflicts of interest?

One example of many abstracts and review articles available at PubMed was titled: **Lactoferrin as potential preventative and adjunct Treatment for Covid-19**. The article was published by Int J Antimicrob Agents. 2020 Sep: 56 Authors: Raymond Chang, Tzi Bun Ng, and Wei-Zen Sun et al.

They wrote:

*"Antivirals and nutritional supplements have been proposed as potentially useful against severe acute respiratory syndrome coronavirus 2 (SARS-CoV-2), the novel coronavirus that causes COVID-19, but few have been clinically established. Lactoferrin (Lf) is a naturally occurring, non-toxic glycoprotein that*

*is orally available as a nutritional supplement and has established in vitro antiviral efficacy against a wide range of viruses, including SARS-CoV, a closely related coronavirus to SARS-CoV-2. Furthermore, Lf possesses unique immunomodulatory and anti-inflammatory effects that may be especially relevant to the pathophysiology of severe COVID-19 cases."*

To date, there are no studies or funding for studies from the NIH or even a review of existing published research by the NIH or the FDA on low cost non-patentable remedies for Covid- 19 - and the same goes for cancer. This failure of FDA doctors and attorneys to read the scientific literature that is available on their computers is just as easily read there as it is on mine. It shows they are mentally incompetent or lazy, are biased regulatory bullies, or, are corrupt with conflicts of interest, and, for any or all of the foregoing reasons they should be promptly fired. For that to happen, the higher-ups in this regulatory food chain must first be honest public servants. It helps if they have a brain, a heart and a spine.

**Historical Note**: More than 2000 years ago, Jesus was breast-fed by his Mother with Colostrum - the first milk from her bosom to her first born Son- a gift from God that provided passive immunity - no jab, no drama, no adverse side effects, no blood clots, and no strokes. Also, no patents or approval from Caesar was needed. Today, as always, women who breastfeed their children can continue to provide this gift of passive immunity to their offspring.

## The story of Cryptosporidium and Colostrum

In 1993, the City of Milwaukee public water supply was contaminated with the parasite cryptosporidium. The contamination sickened over 403,000 residents in Milwaukee County and the City of Milwaukee, Wisconsin. (1) The intestinal infection caused watery diarrhea and caused many deaths. I personally know two people who succumbed to this illness.

When the outbreak was over, Milwaukee Mayor John Norquist searched for a way to prevent this from happening again. He turned his attention to the use of ozone, a disinfectant used in many water treatment systems throughout the world. Ozone is known to kill off cryptosporidium and other water born pathogens. Milwaukee Water Works states that ozone is the city's primary disinfectant. Chlorine is added as a secondary disinfectant.

Mayor John Norquist also visited other cities where they added ozone to the disinfection process with excellent purification results. He obtained most of the original information on Ozonation from the Water Research Foundation.

Since the installation of Ozonation equipment, there has never been another case of cryptosporidium reported from drinking Milwaukee's tap water. Ozone added to water will revert to oxygen in a matter of a few hours.

Ref: 1. Cryptosporidiosis in children during a massive waterborne outbreak in Milwaukee, Wisconsin. Epidemiol Infect. 1997 Aug;119

## Colostrum Specific by Jarrow Formulas

After the cryptosporidium outbreak subsided in 1993, Jarrow Formulas, a dietary supplement company located in California came out with an oral supplement for cryptosporidium made from immunized cows that had been injected with the cryptosporidium parasite. This Colostrum product was rich in anti-bodies also called immuno-globulins and worked very effectively in shortening the duration of a cryptosporidium infection. Surprisingly, the FDA did not attempt to remove this product from the market.

Note: Whole whey protein powder from grass fed cows contains immunoglobulins and lactoferrin but not as much of these immune factors as the first milking known as Colostrum.

## Low Tech Do it Yourself Colostrum

(Sep. 2001) excerpts from Positive Health News

"First, a rectal or hind teat implant of blood and distilled water eliminates the risk of human blood entering the artery vessels of the animal. You can increase the amount of blood from one or 2 drops to 20 drops or more and increase the viral exposure significantly to produce a more potent immunized egg or milk. Third, the membranes of the intestines of the chicken or goat will act like a fine filter to allow the virus to enter the blood stream.

"Minnesota. The **Herb Saunders** method of mammary infusion (the hind teat) while the mammal is pregnant has had 20 years of experience behind it. However, as chickens do not have udders (mammary glands) a colonic infusion is the logical alternative. A syringe with a Cannula sleeve can be used to give either a colonic or mammary gland infusion in a chicken, goat or cow.

"The main reason for using a colonic or mammary gland infusion is the more efficient use of the chicken or goats immune system to produce a potent immunized egg or milk that has only positive effects (antibodies and transfer factors directed only against the pathogens and viruses.

"Robert Carson MD, told me that adding distilled water to blood would lead to a breakdown of the blood cell walls and a release of viral particles into the blood serum. He concurred with the theory that adding distilled water to a few drops of blood might increase the inoculations effectiveness as more viral particles are released from the infected cells. This turned out to be the method that Barbara used."

## Barbara's Test Case

July 25th, 2001. Barbara immunizes her goat to treat her HIV condition. The inoculation sets off an immune reaction fireworks. Somewhere on the East coast of the United States the planned immunization of a goat with HIV-infected blood from one of our readers proceded. Barbara was diagnosed with AIDS about 5 years ago in 1996. Before immunizing her goat, she had blood drawn for lab tests on July 23rd. Her numbers were sobering. CD4 count was 21 and her viral load for HIV was listed in excess of 500,000. This is because the test used only measures up to a 500,000 viral load.

Last month, Barbara, who lives on 2 and 1/2 acres with her 5 children, had planned to infuse her blood in the hind teat of the goat using a syringe with an attached Teat Infusion Cannula. On Wednesday, July 25th, at 9 am, she pricked her finger and drew out about 6 drops of blood that she added to about 1/2 teaspoon of distilled water.

She drew the blood and water mixture into a 3 CC needle syringe. Then she placed the Cannula over the needle and inserted the Cannula into one of the hind teats of the goat. As she began pressing on the syringe plunger, the blood and water mixture started coming out of the bottom of the Cannula instead of going into the udder.

Seeing that this method was not working, she withdrew the syringe and Cannula from the udder and looked for an area of loose skin on the goat to inject the animal subcutaneously. She found a spot on the left side, midsection near the belly that had some loose skin. She inserted the needle at an angle and injected the blood and water mixture under the skin. Immediately, the goat began to dance and stomp around feeling it had been bit. She injected the full 3 cc that was in the syringe.

After the inoculation was over, she noticed that the needle was removable from the syringe and that the Cannula fit over a tube that the needle had occupied. Never having used a Cannula before is why the teat infusion attempt failed. Never-the-less, with the subcutaneous injection, the goat was now exposed to the HIV in her blood and events would soon take their course. She called me shortly after doing the immunization of the goat to tell me what had transpired.

The sign she was waiting for was for the goat to develop a fever. I told Barbara that there would not be any immune modulating value to the milk until this happened. I said: *"with the chickens in Brazil, it took 7 to 10 days before the eggs started producing immune reactions, so I wouldn't expect anything to happen too soon."*

On Thursday morning, July 26th, Barbara called to tell me that by 7 pm Wednesday evening, just 10 hours after the inoculation, the goat was showing signs of being heated and was feeling hot. She said: *"the goat had a major fever last night. My first reaction was one of complete surprise. I had expected a reaction from the goat, but not this soon, and not on the same day of the inoculation."*

I inquired as to how the goat was doing this morning. She said the goat was not as lively as it usually is. It is eating less and acting tired. After we got off the phone, Barbara drank her first cup of milk that she had obtained from the goat on Wednesday evening at the same time the goat was breaking with a fever. Later that day, only a few hours after drinking the first glass of immunized milk, she called to report that she too had developed a low grade fever. It was Thursday evening and this story was just beginning to unfold. For the next several days, she would drink one cup of goat's milk in the morning, the milk having been drawn on the previous day. With strong reactions setting in, there was no need to up the dosage.

On Friday morning, I called Barb to see how she was doing and she reported that she had developed night sweats last night and had not had these in years. She had a headache, her nose was running, her muscles were aching and her throat was sore. She said her temp was just over 100° F. I told her that these were flu-like symptoms and a sign of strong immune activation and that her symptoms were similar to Jose's in Brazil, except hers were much more intense.

Saturday, July 28th: Barbara said that Friday night was kind of scary. Her temperature reached nearly 102° F and she sweated profusely in bed until by 3 am in the morning; the sheets were saturated. She had a pounding headache along with aching muscles. Late Friday evening, doubts began to set in as to whether she should have started this experiment and she prayed and asked God for a sign if she should continue. On Saturday morning, she told me that her head felt "clear" for the first time in years. She took that as a sign to continue.

She continued to drink one cup of the goats milk each morning from the previous days milking and all the symptoms persisted but slightly less intense on Saturday evening and Sunday evening. On Sunday, she reported that her urine turned brown in color and emitted a very strong odor. By Monday morning, the headaches stopped and the aching muscles were gone and the color of the urine had returned to normal - clear and slightly yellow.

By Tuesday morning, her appetite was returning and she began eating normally. However, a few hours after her morning drink of the goat's milk, a low grade fever will develop. By late evening each day, the temperature will reach 101 or 102° F. When it reaches 102, she takes a Tylenol and it drops about 1 degree.

On Thursday, August 2nd, the night sweats stopped. This morning, August 3rd, the 9th day into this experiment, Barbara reports that the only symptom remaining is the fevers that are most noticeable in the evening. In the morning, her temperature is either normal or just slightly elevated. She continues to eat normally and has no more headaches, night sweats or aching muscles.

## The Herb Saunders Method of Immunizing a Cow

Saunders implanted about one teaspoon of blood in each of the two hind teats of cows that were pregnant about 6 to 8 weeks before the calves were expected. He used a hypodermic needle that had a plastic sleeve over it called a "Cannula" and after drawing blood in the syringe would inject it into the udder of the two teats. Saunders said that the cow would develop a fever within a week or two. When the calf is born, the first 2 or 3 milking called Colostrum were saved and frozen in ice cube trays. About 2 cubes were thawed out and used daily.

[In an interview with Herb Saunders in the late 1990's, he told me that in 20 years he seen the use of this Colostrum specific method effectively treat, even cure, any disease including cancer if the people took the Colostrum product for about 3 months.]

## The Pin-prick method of immunizing chickens (Spring 2001)

In a second experiment and as a back-up to the goat, Barbara immunized two chickens by placing a drop of her blood on the chickens and then use a sewing needle that was placed in the middle of the drop of blood to puncture the skin. The puncture was made at a narrow angle about 1/4 inch long so it enters just under the skin like a sliver of wood. The needle was withdrawn after the first puncture and a small amount of blood placed on the tip and then re-inserted into the puncture hole to force a portion of a drop of blood under the skin.

The technique of a needle and a drop of blood is similar to how a doctor might pick up an infection from one of his patients in a hospital when a drop of blood accidentally touches his skin. If the skin has a cut or puncture, it is highly likely that the infection will be transferred. Preventing accidental exposure to a patient's blood is one of the headaches of today's surgeons.

Low-tech methods such as the Saunders method or the Pin-prick method could be done by just about anyone who knows how to read. Once the host animal is exposed to the blood of an infected patient, it may take 2 to 6 weeks or longer for enough viral replication to occur to trigger a systemic immune response in the animal. After this occurs, the milk of a goat or the egg yolk of the chicken will have some real medicinal value.

## For the Teat Infusion Cannula, see a local Veterinarian for Help

The Cannula called a "Teat Infusion Cannula" can be obtained at www.valleyvet.com. Valley Vet Supply, 1118 Pony Express Hwy, Marysville, KS 66508 800-360-4838. The product number is 16439. Cost is $4.25 for 100 plastic cannulas. The web site also list Dr. Larson Plastic Teat Tubes.

## Shelia's Story on eating Raw Eggs

April 18, 2001. a reader with HIV reports on the effects of eating a raw egg for one year. As I was making my final changes to this article on immunizing chickens, the phone rang and I talked with a long term HIV survivor, names Shelia, who has been HIV + since 1988. She has never used prescription drugs all these years. No PCR test was taken in the past 4 years. In 1996, viral load was 20,000. Her CD4 test of two weeks ago was 258.

I thought that this was a rather high number of CD4's to have after being HIV+ for 13 years so I inquired further. I asked her in what year since 1988 did she feel her best. She said it was 1993. I asked: What did you do during that year? Without mentioning to her at the time I was writing this article on immunized eggs, she said: *"Every day I blended a handful of fresh sprouted seeds with one raw egg (organic). I would add some digestive enzymes and drink this. I did this for about one year...My skin glowed. I never felt better."*

Did you ever pick-up a salmonella infection from eating raw eggs during the year? She said; *"No, I did not. It could be because I only used organic eggs."* I asked her if she felt so good drinking this mixture every day, why did she stop? She said it was because she was doing so many different things and grew tired of it all. I inquired further if she had any lab results during this year. She said *"No, as long as I am feeling good, I stay away from doctors."*

In 1994, she got married and in 1996 had a child. She was under tremendous pressure to take drugs to stop the HIV virus for infecting the child, but resisted. I asked her: Is the child OK? She replied: "The child is very healthy and was born HIV negative."

There are several more case reports of persons with HCV (hepatitis C) that used either immunized Colostrum from cows or goats or immunized eggs and reported very good results. As for Coronaviruses, it is highly likely that cows and goats, even chickens, have been exposed to various wild strains of coronaviruses over their lifetime and would have some immune factors that could be transferred to their offspring or to people who wanted the immune enhancing benefits of Colostrum or immunized eggs or both.

## Sources of Colostrum and Immune Transfer Factors

While the FDA and the FTC are busy suppressing information from distributors and manufacturers of Colostrum's health benefits for Covid-19 and other types of infections including cancer, I have prepared the following list of sources of Colostrum with no preference or conflict of interest on my part. Organic eggs are another source of antibodies and transfer factors.

1. Jarrow Formulas **https://jarrow.com  310-204-6936**

Jarrow products - **Colostrum Prime Life** and **LactoFerrin**

2. Sovereign Health **https://sovereignhealthlaboratories.com** 928-202-4031 Products: **Colostrum powder or capsules**.

3. **amosmillerorganicfarm.com**- PA 717-556-0672 An Amish farm that sells fresh frozen Colostrum from a variety of farm animals(cows, buffalo, goats, camels etc). They have the least processed and lowest prices of any source I have located on the internet. Join online as a member and pickup products from several locations listed on their website. Currently, their products

are under the threat of being regulated out of business by the Dept. of Ag. whose polices favor big businesses. The Amish farm Colostrum products are sold by the pint and shipped frozen.

4. **Organic free range pastured eggs** are a natural source of antibodies and other immune factors found the yolks that support a stronger immune system not only for chickens but for pets and humans as well. However, the yolks must not be cooked. Eggs from pastured hens will have dark orange yolk where grain fed hens will have pale yellow yolk.

**Important**: to get the full benefits from an organic egg, the egg yolk must be liquid when you are done cooking it. The egg must never be fried, hard-boiled or scrambled. Overheating will destroy the immune factors in the yolk. There are two ways to do this. It is not necessary to eat a whole raw egg every day.

One is to lightly poach the egg and stop when a slight film over the yolk begins to turn white. The second method is to bring a small pot of water to a boil. Turn off the heat and add one or two pastured eggs to the pot. Bring the water back to a slight boil and simmer the eggs for 4 minutes and then shut off the heat. Wait one minute and then drain all the water and replace it with cold water. Let it stand for another minute or two, then tap the egg shells with a spoon until the shell cracks and gently remove its contents to a dish for eating. You may serve it as is, or on toast, or with mashed potatoes. Enjoy!

**Question**: Will any colostrum or pasteurized egg work as good as one from a mammal that is directly exposed to the viruses or health condition I have?

**Answer**: Probably not. However, there are so many immune factors in Colostrum and raw or partially cooked egg yolks, that you will never know whether or not there are benefits to be derived unless you try it.

It is a fact that FDA approval is no guarantee a drug is safe and effective, although they claim it is. The drug companies will not guarantee cures for their products either. Neither the FDA nor the drug companies will give you your money back if you are not satisfied. In other words, FDA approval or not, every treatment is experimental and no one puts their money where their mouth is.

# Conflicts of interest and Corruption in Washington

There are ongoing conflict of interest between big campaign contributors, (banks, drug companies, chemical companies etc) and regulatory agencies of the Federal Government in Washington DC where laws and regulations are too often written by lobbyists who represent major campaign contributors.

Regulatory agencies whose opinions can no longer be taken at face value include the U.S. Food and Drug Administration (FDA), the National Institute of Health (NIH), the Federal Trade Commission (FTC), the Dept. of Agriculture (DOA), and sadly, even the Dept. of Justice (DOJ). This is only a partial list as big money and corporate influence has created conflicts of interest and outright corruption all over Washington, DC in both major political parties.

It is a fact that some FDA approved "scientific studies" are flawed in their conclusions as the volunteers picked by the drug companies for their studies are often the healthiest of the herd. Persons with preexisting conditions who are taking several prescribed drugs are nearly always excluded from controlled studies. Why? Drug companies have learned long ago that testing a new drug in a patient already over-medicated gives bad results. The problem with all randomized controlled trials (RCTs) is when a dishonest person is involved in a study design, they will figure out a way to cheat and rig the results for financial gain.

If a drug company in the United States has to go to a foreign country to find enough healthy people for a study, they should only be allowed to sell their drug in the country where the study was done. Drug companies doing studies in foreign countries should not be allowed to sell these drugs in the United States.

## Masking - the Benefits and the Adverse effects

To begin with, not all masks are created equal and not all people's ability to breathe is equal. Like shoes, one size does not fit all. There are benefits to using masks short term in reducing the exchange and transmission of airborne viral particles like the coronavirus, the common cold or flu virus. By short term, I mean if you are visiting someone for 30 minutes or less and you want to avoid either getting or transmitting a virus between yourself and the other person, then it makes sense to wear a mask. It is impractical to get a whole nation of millions of people to do this week after week and month after month.

If you know there is a real risk of viral transmission, then you may want the most restrictive facial mask there is - the N95 or surgical mask for use for 10 or 15 minutes but definitely not all day. Regular cloth masks may look pretty but they mainly divert exhaled particles sideways with some passing through the center of the mask. In May of 2020, I read the sign of one person who was protesting the mandatory masking and shutdowns that stated, in paraphrasing Patrick Henry: *"Give me liberty or give me Covid-19."*

## The N95 mask reduces air-flow and oxygen

The N95 mask is sometimes called a surgical mask. The N95 mask fits tightly against the face of the person wearing it. This makes breathing harder for the masked person. In 2011 in a small study on 14 people published in *The Annals of Occupational Hygiene* (1) the authors Heow Pueh Lee and De Yun Wang found that -

*"The results showed a mean increment of 126 and 122% in inspiratory and expiratory flow resistances, respectively, with the use of N95 respirators. There was also an average reduction of 37% in air exchange volume with the use of N95 respirators. This is the first reported study that demonstrates quantitatively and objectively the substantial impairment of nasal airflow in terms of increased breathing resistance with the use of N95 respirators on actual human subjects."* (1)

Ref:

1. Objective Assessment of increase in Breathing Resistance of N95 Respirators on Human Subjects. Annals of Occupational Hygiene Vol. 55 No 8 Oct, 2011. Pages 917 - 921

Editor's comment: Some of the published studies that whitewash the adverse effects of masks and especially the N95 mask are conveniently designed to test them for a short amount of time. Studies designed for a predetermined result are for marketing and propaganda purposes only. The truth comes out when the mask is tested under the stress conditions of work and movement where saliva and spit will build up inside the masks over an extended period of time (e.g. 8 hours). The moisture buildup inside a mask will hinder airflow and oxygen intake and this is time dependent.

It is truly amazing how some big corporations can pull the wool over the public's eyes while at the same time pulling the masks over our mouths. Many doctors who fail to think critically are misled by these disinformation campaigns.

A simple device that you can put over your finger will measure oxygen levels in the blood. It is called an **Oximeter** and costs less than $20. Test your oxygen levels at the beginning of a day and at the end while the mask is still on to measure drops or changes in blood oxygen levels. When the mask becomes moist inside with spit or saliva, it will reduce airflow and thus impact your oxygen levels negatively.

With reduced blood oxygen levels will be an increase in the heart rate and a shift in the blood pH to the acidic side. Short term testing of the N95 mask under laboratory conditions can give you misleading results as to the safety of long-term use of the mask.

## Local Priest passes out using the N95 mask

On Sunday June 28, 2020, Father Allan told the parishioners of Mary Queen of Heaven Church that he almost collapsed giving a eulogy at a recent funeral. He said he was wearing the N95 mask at the time and had to stop for a minute and pull the mask down his face to get a breath of fresh air and regain his full consciousness. Why are there no warnings that come with the N95 mask to avoid gradual suffocation (hypoxia) if you wear it too long or build up saliva and spit inside the mask that further hinders air-flow and oxygen to your lungs?

## Emotional Stress - the price of social distancing

The transmission of viral particles through the center of the mask is pretty much a given which leads to the next restriction on human behavior - social distancing of 6 ft. The effects of social distancing take a terrible toll on all of society but especially children, single people of any age, and the elderly. It takes all the fun out of living. It brings on long periods of loneliness, mental and emotional depression.

When this goes on for month after month, you can understand the pain of isolation for a prisoner in solitary confinement. For an entire city, state or nation to live like this indefinitely is inhumane and the whole of society becomes a prison. It is an abuse of laws and regulations, especially for children, single people and the elderly.

## Avoid vaccines when using immunosuppressive drugs

Many ads for drugs listed here tell you not to use them if you plan on getting a vaccine or have an infection. What they should also tell you is that if you get a vaccine while using an immuno-suppressive drug that the antibody response you want from the vaccine may fail to materialize. In other words the vaccine fails and you still have serious adverse side effects.

Immunosuppressive drugs are often used to treat psoriasis, lupus, rheumatoid arthritis, crohn's, multiple sclerosis and alopecia. The following list of 17 drugs are advertised on television to not be used with an active infection. This list includes Humira, Tremfya, Rinvoq, Xeljanz, Skyrizi, Cimzia, Enbrel, Simponi, Remicade, Taltz, Tysabri, Rituxan, Cosentyx, Actemra, Stelara, Orencia, and Entyvio.

Note: This list is not complete. Covid-19 should be mentioned by name in these drug ads but the FDA is silent on this critical issue. It could be incompetence or conflicts of interest, or both.

Why are major TV and radio media networks also silent? **The answer is money** - they want the money the ADS bring. To find out if the drug you are taking is immunosuppressive, go to the website **drugs.com** and look up the drugs side effects.

### Did you ever hear of the Rule of 3?

Remember - **The Rule of 3.** You can live 3 weeks without food, 3 days without water but only 3 minutes without oxygen. I don't recall the author of the rule of 3. However, as with all rules, there probably is some wiggle room here, but not a lot.

## Preexisting Conditions are a "Red Flashing Light"

A partial list of conditions in persons who should get their doctor's approval _before_ taking the Covid jab

Asthma
Auto-immune diseases
Blood clotting issues
Bronchitis
Cancer
Chronic Diarrhea
Chronic Fatigue
Chronic Insomnia
Chest pains
COPD
Diabetes types 1 and 2
Dementia - Alzheimers
Emphysema
Heart Disease or palpitations
Hypertension - very high
Multiple Sclerosis
Morbid Obesity
Neuropathy
Organ transplants
Shortness of Breath

## The HIV link to Covid-19

### Iranian Scientists find in computer modeling that six HIV drugs interlock with the Covid-19 coronavirus

On May 21, 2020, an article appeared in thebody.com by Michael Broder about the use of HIV drugs to treat the virus (SARS-CoV-2). The drugs being tested for Covid-19 belong to a class known as protease inhibitors. Protease inhibitors were originally introduced about 25 years ago (1996) in combination with other drugs to treat HIV/AIDS.
Broder stated:

_"Evidence from a docking study in Iran suggests that the six most promising HIV protease inhibitors are likely to be effective against COVID-19 in the following order:_
1. tipranavir

2. indinavir
3. atazanavir
4. darunavir
5. ritonavir
6. amprenavir

*"To date, the HIV treatment that has been most studied in COVID-19 clinical trials is the combination of the HIV protease inhibitors lopinavir and ritonavir, marketed as Kaletra. Kaletra took the lead in the search for COVID-19 treatments because researchers years ago identified it as a promising treatment for severe acute respiratory syndrome, or SARS, and Middle East respiratory syndrome (MERS), two other deadly infections caused by coronaviruses."*

Broder's entire article can be read here:
https://www.thebody.com/article/hiv-drugs-clinical-trials-to-treat-covid-19

## Was HIV spliced into the SARS Coronavirus?

Since it is true that some HIV drugs can inhibit or stop the Coronavirus from replicating, then it is also plausible that part of the virus that causes Covid-19 came from the HIV virus.  This theory would be DOA - dead on arrival if none of the HIV drugs had any anti-Covid-19 effects.

However, since several trials testing HIV drugs are now underway, it raises the next question - how could this possibly have occurred in nature by itself? It seems this marriage between the HIV virus and a cold virus must have had the assistance of researchers who figured out how to merge these two viruses to have a "gain of function."

## Australia Abandons Coronavirus Vaccine After Study Participants Test HIV Positive - December 11, 2020

Australia has cancelled an agreement to distribute 51 million doses of a vaccine made by CSL Limited. The vaccine was abandoned after several persons in the trial receiving the vaccine tested positive with an HIV antibody test.

The Australian Prime Minister, Scott Morrison, stated:

*"University of Queensland vaccine will not be able to proceed based on the scientific advice, and that will no longer feature as part of*

*Australia's vaccine plan."*

CSL Ltd used the Covid-19 *"spike protein"* technology for vaccine research using molecular clamp technology to lock the protein into a shape that allows the immune system to be able to recognize and then neutralize the virus.

Mike Ives of the New York Times reported the following on Dec 11, 2020:

*"The trouble that arose with the Australian vaccine, developed by the University of Queensland and the biotech company CSL, was related to its use of two fragments of a protein found in H.I.V.*

*"The protein formed part of a molecular "clamp" that researchers placed on the spikes that surround the coronavirus and allow it to enter healthy cells. The clamp stabilizes the spikes, allowing the immune system to respond more effectively to the vaccine.*

*"The use of the H.I.V. protein posed no risk of infecting the volunteers with that virus, the researchers said. But the clamp generated the production of antibodies recognized by H.I.V. tests at higher levels than the scientists had expected."*

Editor's comment: One could surmise that the FDA and NIH would not want widespread use of generic HIV drugs to treat Covid-19 for three reasons.

1. It would raise concern that Covid-19 is a man-made airborne form of HIV spread through the air.

2. Although Covid-19 is not exactly the same as HIV, the HIV drugs could have saved millions of lives by shortening recovery time from Covid even when the patients are elderly or immune-compromised. Why did they not use them?

3. For the same reason the drug companies do not want government money spent on research for low cost remedies for Covid-19, they also do not want low cost treatment for cancer or any other disease. There is clearly more money to be made with the vaccines or patented drugs where the drug company is granted a patent and an FDA market monopoly for 17 years with no legal limits on the prices they charge. Congress could do something about this but won't as long as they continue to accept money from big Pharma in the form of campaign contributions.

# TREATMENTS
## Covid Treatments used in Hospitals

**Regeneron** - casirivimab/imdevimab antibodies administered i.v.
**Dexamethasone** - anti-inflammatory
**Tocilizumab** is a lab-generated antibody that blocks the interleukin-6 pathway
**Covalent Plasma** - antibodies and immune factors from patients who have recovered from Covid-19 - highly effective.
**I.C.U. Ventilators** and **Supplemental Oxygen**
**UV light** - could be used in ventilation systems in hospitals to reduce viral particles in the air and in the patient's room. the alternative is to bring the patients outside for some fresh air and sunlight.

Remdesivir is an FDA approved antiviral drug for HCV that has not proved helpful. On Nov 20, 2020, the World Health Organization (WHO), one month after the FDA approved Gileads Remdesivir for Covid, stated the drug has *"no meaningful effect on mortality or on other important outcomes for patients."*

**Author's suggestions** for hospitals - One of the most valuable treatments for Covid-19 is hidden in plain sight. It is hydrogen peroxide. Place clean cotton socks on patients and pour 1/4 cup of **3% hydrogen peroxide** solution slowly over each sock. Repeat this treatment every 8 hours. The hydrogen peroxide will be absorbed into the blood stream through the feet and kill off the Covid-19 viruses in the blood. Most of the patients will recover and go home instead of remaining in the hospital.

It also helps to remove all masks from patients and replace them with supplemental oxygen or replace the cotton or cloth masks hourly to remove moisture buildup. Any mask, but especially the N95 masks, will kill off many of your patients and some doctors who will also develop heart palpitations from their use.

## Repurposed drugs to treat Covid-19

**Ivermectin** - powerful antiviral (Prescription required).
**Hydroxychloroquine** (HCQ) - anti-inflammtory (Prescription required for 200 mg tablets called Plaquenil). or use **Cinchona**

**bark** capsules. No Prescription required- Cinchona bark contains natural quinine and natural co-factors. The dose is 2 capsules twice a day for the first 3 days then reduce to 2 capsules each day for 14 days or as advised by a doctor. For Cinchona bark capsules, search online or contact the Penn Herb Co at 215-632-6200 **pennherb.com**

**Note:** Quinine from Cinchona bark is also used to flavor **Tonic Water** and is sold in liquor stores.

**HIV drugs** - generic brands like **kaletra/epivir** are a safe and effective choice for anyone with Covid-19. Shame on the FDA for not giving Emergency Use Authorization for doctors to prescribe kaletra/epivir combo or other HIV combos for thousands of elderly people who have Covid-19.

### Ivermectin - a Safe Remedy by Dr. Pierre Kory MD

The following are excerpts of testimony of Dr. Pierre Kory MD before Senator Ron Johnson's Homeland Security Meeting on Alternative treatments for Covid -19 on Dec 8, 2020

*"I am speaking today not only as an individual physician, but also on behalf of my non-profit organization, the Front-Line COVID-19 Critical Care Alliance, (http://www.flccc.net) made up of some of the most highly published and well-known critical care experts in the world with almost 2,000 peer -reviewed publications in the medical literature as well as over 100 years of bedside clinical experience in ICU's around the country........*

*"it is with great pride as well as significant optimism, that I am here to report that our group, led by Professor Paul E. Marik, has developed a highly effective protocol for preventing and early treatment of COVID-19. In the last 3-4 months, emerging publications provide conclusive data on the profound efficacy of the anti-parasite, anti-viral drug, anti-inflammatory agent called ivermectin in all stages of the disease.*

*"Before proceeding, I want to bring attention to two critical deficits in our national treatment response that has made this hearing necessary in the first place. Besides the early interest and research into hydroxychloroquine, we can find no other significant efforts to research the use of any other already existing, safe, low-cost therapeutic agents.*

*"Seemingly the only research and treatment focus that we have observed on a national scale is with novel or high-cost pharmaceutically*

engineered products such as remdesivir, monoclonal antibodies, tocilizumab, with all such therapies costing thousands of dollars. This is consistent with conclusions drawn by a physician consulting to Congress about Covid-19 when she concluded,

"There is a pervasive problem on the Hill with how we prove the value of a low cost treatment." Another barrier has been the censorship of all of our attempts at disseminating critical scientific information on Facebook and other social media with our pages repeatedly being blocked......

"Ivermectin is highly safe, widely available, and low cost. Its discovery was awarded the Nobel Prize in medicine, and is already included on the WHO's "World's List of Essential Medicines." We now have data from over 20 well-designed clinical studies, ten of them randomized, controlled trials, with every study consistently reporting large magnitude and statistically significant benefits in decreasing transmission rates, shortening recovery times, decreasing hospitalizations, or large reductions in deaths.

"This clinical data is also supported by multiple basic science, in-vitro and animal studies. Our manuscript, completed one week ago, is already out of date due to the near daily emergence of new, positive ivermectin studies. The manuscript has been posted on the medical pre-print server OSF (Open Science Foundation) and can be downloaded on our organization's website, **www.flccc.net.**

"A more updated meta-analysis and review authored by a group of Ph.D. researchers and scientists includes all ivermectin studies as of December 4th, 2020 and can be found on the c19study.com website here: https://ivmmeta.com/

"These data show that ivermectin is effectively a "miracle drug" against COVID-19. The magnitude of the effect is similar to its Nobel prize-worthy historical impacts against parasitic disease across many parts of the globe.....

"Ivermectin is already eradicating coronavirus infections in multiple regions of the world. Dozens of studies demonstrate its efficacy from studies done from "bench to the bedside" as follows:

1) Since 2012, multiple in-vitro studies have demonstrated that Ivermectin inhibits the replication of many viruses, including influenza, Zika, Dengue and others (19-27).

2) Ivermectin inhibits SARS-CoV-2 replication, leading to the absence of nearly all viral material by 48h in infected cell cultures (28).

3)  Ivermectin has potent anti-inflammatory properties with in-vitro data demonstrating profound inhibition of both cytokine production and transcription of nuclear factor-kB (NF-kB), the most potent mediator of inflammation (29-31).
4)  Ivermectin significantly diminishes viral load and protects against organ damage in multiple animal models when infected with SARS-CoV-2 or similar coronaviruses (32, 33).
5)  Ivermectin prevents transmission and development of COVID-19 disease in those exposed to infected patients (34-36,54,88).
6)  Ivermectin hastens recovery and prevents deterioration in patients with mild to moderate disease treated early after symptoms (37-42,54).
7)  Ivermectin hastens recovery and avoidance of ICU admission and death in hospitalized patients (40,43,45,54,63,67).
8)  Ivermectin reduces mortality in critically ill patients with COVID-19 (43,45,54).
9)  Ivermectin leads to striking reductions in case-fatality rates in regions with widespread use (46-48).
10) The safety of ivermectin is nearly unparalleled given its near nil drug interactions along with only mild and rare side effects observed in almost 40 years of use and billions of doses administered (49).
11) The World Health Organization has long included ivermectin on its "List of Essential Medicines" (50).

## MEDICATION RECOMMENDED by Dr Pierre Kory MD

[Note- Ivermectin comes in 3 mg pills. A dose is 3 mg per 30 lbs of body weight. A person weighing 180 lbs would need 6 tablets on day one and 6 more tablets on day 3. The tablets are taken all at once with water or juice.]

**Ivermectin** 0.2 mg/kg* dose on day 1 and day 3,
Vitamin D3 - 1000 i.u to 3000 i.u daily [Consider Cod Liver oil- 2 caps 2 X Blue Ice brand by greenpastures.org]
Vitamin C 1000 mg twice daily
Quercetin - 250 mg/day
Melatonin 6 mg before bedtime (causes drowsiness)
Zinc 50 mg/day of elemental zinc

For treating advanced cases of Covid-19 that require hospitalization go to **www.flccc.net** for more information.

**References and Notes**
1.  Front Line COVID-19 Critical Care Working Group. MATH+ hospital treatment

protcol for COVID-19. www.flccc.net. (2020).
2.  E. Marik, P. Kory, J. Varon, J. Iglesias, G. U. Meduri, MATH+ protocol for the treatment of SARS-CoV-2 infection: the scientific rationale. Expert Review of Anti-infective Therapy. 10.1080/14787210.2020.1808462 (2020).
3.  P. Kory, G. U. Meduri, J Iglesias, J. Varon, P. E. Marik. Clinical and scientific rationale for the MATH+ hospital treatment protocol for COVID-19. J Int Care Med. (2020)

## **Hydroxychloroquine** (HCQ) or **Cinchona bark** capsules.

HCQ is a FDA approved synthetic form of quinine that has been in use since the 1940's. It is approved for treatment of malaria. Both HCQ and Cinchona are powerful anti-inflammatories and have been used to treat the same health conditions. Either HCQ or Cinchona bark capsules may be used in combination with Ivermectin for synergistic results. From the Keep Hope Alive Journal- Vol 18 N3 is excerpted the following:

"Most of the national media's attention has been focused on the synthetic forms of quinine known as chloroquine and hydroxychloroquine used around the world since 1944 in the treatment of Malaria, Lupus, Rheumatoid Arthritis and other auto immune diseases as well as Covid-19. The benefits seem to be in the anti-inflammatory category. Natural quinine in Cinchona bark or Tonic water has also been used to treat leg cramps.

"While I have disagreements with President Trump on other issues, I do agree with his promotion of the use of hydroxychloroquine for shortening the recovery time from Covid-19. Hydroxychloroquine is a low cost synthetic form of quinine sold under the name Plaquenil and usually comes in 200 mg tablets. For dosing the Journal of Rheumatology recommends 200 mg twice a day for adults with arthritis or rheumatism.

"Cinchona bark may be helpful as an anti-inflammatory for Coronavirus infection to cool down an overactive immune cytokine storm that restricts breathing. Cinchona bark has been used for curing Malaria for the past 4 centuries. It is the original source of quinine used during the 16th, 17th and 18th centuries by Jesuit priests in South America. Cinchona bark in capsules or bulk powder is available and can be purchased online. Use a web browser to find a source. I located the capsules at pennherbs.com 215-632-6100. Note: You can buy a bottle of Tonic Water at a liquor store - it contains quinine, unfortunately sugar also.

# Low Cost Home Remedies

Summary- the fastest recovery strategy is to take a strong antiviral, a strong anti-inflammatory and ACE2 receptor blockers.

## I. Antivirals for SARS-CoV-2
**Hydrogen Peroxide** in bath water or orally - low dose
**Grapefruit Seed** Extract with Wormwood. (Nutribiotic brand)
**Thymol from Thyme** or Oregano (Bronchial Clear by Terry's Naturals.
**Raw Garlic with Sauerkraut**
**Berberine** or **Golden Seal root** capsules

## 2. Anti-inflammatories
**Cayenne**
**Cinchona bark** - the original source of quinine or use HCQ (hydrocychloroquine - prescribed drug)
**L-Glutathione** or **N-Acetyl Cysteine**
**Colostrum or lactoferrin** (ACE2 receptor blockers)
**Whole leaf Aloe Vera juice - (**ACE2 blocker)
**Turmeric or Curcumin**

## ACE2 Blockers of SARS-CoV-2

ACE2 receptor blockers is a simple way to prevent and treat Covid-19 and save lives. ACE2 blood vessel receptor blockers do not have the adverse side effects profile of the vaccines. Substances that block Sars-Cov-2 infection from docking with the ACE2 receptors in the blood vessels, lungs and other organs include **Colostrum**, **lactoferrin** (a component of Colotsrum) and **Aloe-Emodin -** found in **whole leaf aloe vera juice**. New research in Germany has found that **dandelion leaves** also block the ACE2 fusion of SARS-CoV-2

**For intestinal infections** from Covid-19 or multiple other causes - use **sauerkraut with one clove of sliced raw garlic** once or twice a day.

## **Nicotine and or caffeine as ACE2 receptor blockers**

A novel experimental Covid-19 remedy - a cigarette anyone?

As a former smoker, I advise anyone to use this information with caution but to use it if it the only thing readily available in the event you suspect you may have been exposed to the SARS-Cov-2 virus from another person. This advice is to light up a cigarette and smoke the virus out of your sinus and lungs. The airborne virus normally enters your body through your nose. Researchers have found that it stays in the nasal area about two days before migrating to the lungs where it may cause pneumonia.

For this remedy, all you need is **one cigarette.** You inhale the smoke into your lungs but exhale the smoke through your nose. You do this two or 3 times. The nicotine in the smoke is a poison and it kills just about every microbial pathogen in its path including viruses. If you exhale the smoke only through your mouth, you won't kill the Covid-19 virus in your sinus and after you are sleeping the virus will still grow in the sinus and could eventually reach your lungs. Smoking a couple puffs off a cigarette just before bedtime remembering to exhale only through your nose might just be good habit for this pandemic. Here is the research that supports the use of nicotine as well as caffeine.

It was published in the journal "Microorganisms 2020 Oct; 8(10): 1600" in an article by Saeedeh Mohammadi et al titled: In silico Investigation on the Inhibiting Role of Nicotine/Caffeine by Blocking the S Protein of SARS-CoV-2...ACE2 Receptor."

An excerpt from this article reads: *"In China, a systematic review and meta-analysis studies on 5960 currently smoking patients demonstrated that pharmaceutical nicotine should be considered as a potential treatment option in COVID-19 [22]. Also, other investigations have revealed the positive effects of nicotine as a potential treatment for COVID-19 in 6515 patients and has shown that hospitalized current smokers, compared to non-smokers, had higher recovery rates."*

You may search PubMed at the NLM for the entire article. It is free. Note: for a caffeine source, I would recommend green tea over roasted coffee (Green tea is also known for its anti-oxidant benefits). Also, **incense** from smoke used in church services should be investigated for their potential antiviral effects.

# Case Report on Grapefruit seed extract

3/2/20 West Allis, WI

On February 19, 2020, a neighbor rings my doorbell. I opened the door and could immediately tell something was wrong. He looked ill. He told me he had a cold sweat and that he had been vomiting. I offered to take him to a local hospital. He declined my offer. I told him he might have the flu. Then, he said: *"you know I am an atheist and don't believe in God."* He said he was afraid of dying and asked me to pray for him…

I asked him if he wanted try the grapefruit seed extract as I had a bottle of Nutribiotics capsules that I had obtained about 10 years earlier and it was still dated for use. He agreed to try it. I opened one capsule and added it to 4 ounces of water. He drank it and waited. About 30 minutes went by and he said he was holding it down. I then offered to give him a fresh grapefruit seed from one I had in my kitchen and he agreed to try it.

Since my neighbor had no teeth to chew the seed, he swallowed the seed whole with a small glass of water. I wasn't sure what a whole seed would do – it might not break down in his stomach. However, an hour went and the vomiting stopped. The cold sweats also began to diminish. He said he felt 50% better. With his symptoms going away, he went home.

## Case Report - Cayenne pepper stops vascular inflammation & removes blood clots

A report posted at Earthclinic.com on May 11, 2020 that claimed cayenne worked miracles.

Tyler Vincent, Canyon BC wrote:

*"Cayenne capsules are LIFE SAVERS, prevents covid19 induced stroke, heart attack, and blood clots; 70% of fatal cases had blood clot, 40% of ICU and severe home cases have blood clots. Canadian & US doctors prescribe blood thinners to even mild Covid patients, sent back home, to prevent blood clots. ………"*

*"I've had corona, now day 78. I'm 36; I got worst-case corona cytokine storms, which have a 40% mortality rate. On day 58 I took two cayenne capsules, I was not prepared for what was about to happen. I felt the cayenne go into my lungs and completely clear them*

*out. My lung pains and kidney pains are nearly totally gone now."*

*"Cayenne pills come in 350mg up to 500 mg depending on who you buy them from. You will need to take them with food if you have a weak stomach. Or, you can simply mix 1/2 teaspoon cayenne pepper powder in a cup of warm milk. The reason you are using milk is because dairy products are known to "take the heat out of hot peppers". Making it easier to consume. "*

*"If you decide to use pills, do NOT buy them from Walmart "Spring Valley" brand. I bought some and they had a yellow powder in them. I cracked one open to taste the powder and NO HEAT. I don't know what they were but it wasn't cayenne pepper. Found out later that Spring Valley is a Chinese owned company so there you go."*

[Editor's note: Cayenne is an interleukin 6 (IL6) inhibitor.]

## Hydrogen Peroxide and Cayenne

Hydrogen peroxide (H202) and cayenne pepper are the two most important substances to keep in your medicine cabinet to protect you from an assault from the Covid virus including the mutants or variants. Hydrogen peroxide has been used to fight infections of all kinds since it was made publicly available in 1885. The EPA "N list" in 2020 had over 30 products listed that kill coronaviruses with hydrogen peroxide.

**Foot Absorption method**: Small amounts of hydrogen peroxide (H2O2) taken orally or absorbed through the feet have produced good results for a wide range of infections. For absorption though the feet, soak two socks each in 1/4 cup of 3% H2O2. Place on the feet and repeat this treatment twice a day about 8 hours apart. The foot soak method has been highly beneficial for 3 cases of emphysema,

## Case Report on foot absorption of H2O2

Toronto, Canada posted 01/07/21 at earthclinic.com

*"Thank you Conrad for this method of using H2O2 by soaking your feet for 5 minutes. I have sinus issues, and a chest congestion and they bother me a lot. I have tried different nasal sprays both natural and prescription but they work only temporarily. I did soak my feet today and I truly feel a difference. Will keep at it for at least a week and*

*more if necessary, and hopefully I will be healed. Such a great site and such nice people here. Thank you all for sharing and God bless us all.* Diane

**Hydrogen Peroxide in bathwater** method. This has been 100% successful locally here in Wisconsin for two cases of measles and another one of chicken pox. The entire treatment consisted of adding 3 quarts of 3% hydrogen peroxide to a bathtub full of warm water and to soak in it for 20 to 30 minutes. Just one treatment in both these cases resulted in complete cures and no residual scar tissue. More than 30 years ago, 3 persons with emphysema reported healing their lungs by soaking their feet in 3% hydrogen peroxide for 20 to 30 minutes a day.

**The Nebulizer method** of using diluted hydrogen peroxide solution for nasal and lung infection of Covid-19 and or other viruses. Numerous articles published in 2020 and 2021 discuss the need for clinical trials using nebulized H2O2 and water to treat infections in the sinus cavity and the lungs. The dose is one part 3% H2O2 to 2 parts of water or saline solution. It is placed in a nebulizer and inhaled. Do not use 3% H2O2 full strength in a nebulizers for nasal and lung inhalation as it is too strong. Regular 3% H2O2 in the brown bottle may also be used as a mouth rinse and throat gargle. Food grade 3% that is diluted to 1% may be used in a nebulizer or taken orally according to directions.

**Hydrogen Peroxide** in a Humidifier. Add 1 tablespoon of 3% hydrogen peroxide to each 3 gallons of water in a humidifier.

## I.V. hydrogen peroxide used to cure terminal patients of the 1920 world influenza pandemic

The following is an excerpt from The Lancet, Feb 21, 1920. The article is **Influenzal Pneumonia: The Intravenous Injection of Hydrogen Peroxide** by T Oliver and D. Murphy et al.

They first treated one terminal patient with low dose i.v. hydrogen peroxide and the patient recovered. They did it slowly and stopped the infusion for half a minute every 4 minutes to avoided creating a gas embolism. The long and short of this story is that the patient fully recovered. The doctors then tried the same treatment on 24 more terminal or hopeless influenzal patients. Of the 24 they treated, 12 died and 13 recovered. Considering that all 24 were terminal patients, the recoveries were remarkable.

A full reprint of the Lancet article and the exact method they used for the infusions can be accessed in a link in the footnotes at *orthmolecular.org in an article by Dr Thomas Levy MD from July 2020 titled: **Covid-19 How Can I cure Thee? Let Me Count the Ways.** The article discusses 14 ways to prevent treat, or even cure Covid-19. A link to find an orthomolecular doctor near you is also provided. *Ref: orthomolecular.org

## Serrapeptase enzymes dissolves old blood clots

Serrapeptase is an enzyme used by silkworms to dissolve their cocoons. Serrapeptase is used to dissolve old blood clots, reverse hardening of the arteries, and back pain. (1)

Serrapeptase is used for painful conditions including back pain, osteoarthritis, reduces pain and swellings including vein swelling, varicose veins, atherosclerosis or hardening of the arteries, various intestinal conditions where inflammatory symptoms exist.

Nursing mothers have also used it for breast pain and it has been used for fibroid tumors. Serrapeptase is sold in health food stores and online. Both cayenne and Serrapeptase will be very valuable for Covid long haulers to help restore circulation and regain use of your brain and limbs.

1. webmd.com
2. pubmed - duckduckgo or google for this site.

## Self-Immunization with Hydrogen Peroxide

**Hydrogen Peroxide in bath water method**. Fill a bath tub with warm water not higher than 105 degrees F. Add 3 quarts of 3% hydrogen peroxide to the bath water. Set a timer for 20 minutes. Have someone watch you or check on you so you don't fall asleep in the tub. Repeat this every other day for 3 days. (Example: Mon, Weds and Fri) Repeat the treatment if the virus does not clear with standard lab tests. Have your doctor take a stool specimen test for Covid-19 if you have any intestinal urbances (diarrhea, knots, cramps, small diameter or sinking ools). Use the Diet plan in this booklet with particular attention to using fermented foods (the sauerkraut and raw garlic snack).

## Oral Use of Food Grade Hydrogen Peroxide.

For short term use of H2O2 for 5 to 7 days, and after consultation with your doctor, add 1 teaspoon of 3% food grade H2O2 to an 8 ounce glass of water and drink this once every 2 hours up to 6 times a day. Food grade 3% H2O2 is sold in many health food stores. Food grade quality H2O2 in higher concentrations is also available in health food stores and some pharmacies. The food grade quality tastes better than the H2O2 in the brown bottle.

The dose will need to be reduced as the concentration increases. The following are equivalents: 1 teaspoon of 3% H2O2 equals 1/2 tsp. of 6% = 1/4 tsp. of 12% = 7 drops of 35% H2O2 solution. These doses must always be added to water or fruit juice before being taken orally. Do not take H2O2 with iron pills or free radicals will form and give you a sore stomach. For more information, see the two books referenced below (1, 2).
1. Hydrogen Peroxide -Medical Miracle by Dr. William C Douglass MD.
2. Hydrogen Peroxide and Aloe Vera by Conrad LeBeau - available at lebeaubooks.com

## Cayenne prevents and dissolves blood clots

Cayenne powder or capsules will both prevent and dissolve blood clots. However, with blood clots, it is both foolish and dangerous to wait until you have blood clots to begin taking it. Just one blood clot could leave you paralyzed or give you a stroke that kills you. Covid-19 and some of the vaccines currently being distributed have caused blood clots that have crippled or killed people. This is because the spike protein on the virus attaches to the ACE2 receptor in the blood vessels. Both hydrogen peroxide and cayenne will counter the adverse effects of both Covid-19 and the current vaccines being used.

If your doctor prescribes blood thinners, it is wise to consult with him about also taking cayenne as a blood thinner and remedy to prevent or dissolve newly formed blood clots. Most cayenne capsules contain around 500 mg which is the equivalent to 1/4 teaspoon of cayenne powder. One cayenne capsule taken with either food or a glass of water 3 times a day should be sufficient for most purposes.

If you take cayenne to prevent a blood clot from a vaccine, it is best to start doing this one day before the vaccination and to continue this for about 14 days, after which one cayenne capsule a day should be sufficient for preventive purposes.

## Covid-19 Long Haulers

The symptoms were reported by Chris Cuomo on CNN a few weeks ago as brain fog, fatigue, depression, memory loss, and shortness of breath. According to Chris Cuomo whose brother is the governor of New York State, "*doctors don't what causes or how to help the Covid long haulers.*" Chris and his wife are public about their own encounter and recovery from Covid-19. There are now support groups that have formed or are forming in numerous states. Use your browser and search "support groups for covid-19" or use Facebook or other social media to ask how to connect with others. The following website was started by Dr. Francis Collins. He lists 10 top Symptoms for long haulers.
https://directorsblog.nih.gov/tag/body-politic-covid-19-support-group

## Long Hauler Symptoms

"Top 10 Symptoms: Respondents were asked to rank their most common symptoms and their relative severity. From highest to lowest, they were: mild shortness of breath, mild tightness of chest, moderate fatigue, mild fatigue, chills or sweats, mild body aches, dry cough, elevated temperature (98.8-100), mild headache, and brain fog/concentration challenges. .....
Highlighting the value of patient-led research, the team was able to assemble an initial list of 62 symptoms that long-haulers often discuss in support groups. The survey revealed common symptoms that have been greatly underreported in the media, such as neurological symptoms. These include brain fog, concentration challenges, and dizziness."

# 8 Helpful Remedies for persons living with Covid-19 long haulers symptoms or with vaccine side effects

1. **35% H2O2** Consider 7 drops of 35% H2O2 added to a glass of water and use this anytime you feel tightness in the chest area. Repeat once every 2 to 4 hours for 3 to 5 days per week or as needed or directed. (H2O2 kills viruses)

2. **Cayenne**. Consider the daily use of **cayenne.** Take one capsule 2 or 3 times a day with meals. Dissolves blood clots

3. **Serrapeptase** enyymes- originally used by silkworms to dissolve their cocoons. Serrapeptase dissolves old blood clots and scar tissue. Take 1 or 2 caps daily as directed.

4. **Colostrum** - to protect the ACE2 blood receptors from the Covid spike protein. (blocks Covid-19 viral activity in blood vessels)

5. **Berberine** or **Golden Seal Root** capsules - take as directed on label. (kills viruses)

6. **Garlic** - 1 clove with meals or with sauerkraut or gluten free whole grain crackers or bread. (anti-viral, anti cancer, supports T cell immunity)

7. **Aromatherapy** - 3 to 6 peeled raw **Garlic toes** poked with a fork and placed in a small clean sock - place near your mouth or nose while sleeping or resting indoors on a recliner or sofa. Inhale deeply. One garlic toe can be poked with a fork and held near the nostril while deeply inhaling for anti viral benefits. Other spices for aromatherapy include the spice **Cloves** and also **Lemon eucalyptus.** Buy a half pound of cloves and place is a thin cloth bag or bowl near the person who is ill. Lemon eucalyptus can also be sprayed on a small cloth and inhaled.

8. **Castor oil pack over the chest area with heat pad**- This Edgar Casey remedy will work miracles in clearing the lungs of viruses and scar tissue.

To prepare a castor oil pack for your chest area, you need an electric heat pad with an adjustable temp control switch. Size should be about 12" x 12". Also buy one pint or quart of castor oil. One roll of aluminum foil. A pack of 12 X 12 terry cotton cloths.

Place heat pad on table and turn on heat. Tear off a 12 X 12 piece of aluminum foil and place on top of heat pad and place the cotton cloth on top. Pour 1/4 cup of castor oil on the terry cloth. Also get a large bath towel. After 5 to 10 minutes of preheating, pick up the heat pad and while holding the layers together, place the castor oil soaked cotton cloth on your chest area and the wrap the bath towel all around your chest area and tuck in your back. Do this treatment for one hour and adjust the heat up or down to a comfortable level.

When done, massage any castor oil not absorbed into your chest. When you feel you are done rinse and wipe off your chest with soap and water or use a shower. Try to avoid getting the oil on the furniture; if you do, rub it off with warm soap and water and a new towel. It is advisable not to reuse the cotton terry cloth. You can buy a packet of them at a local hardware store so it is convenient to use them just once.

## Sauerkraut and Garlic for the Flu or Covid-19

I have had personal success in warding off stomach and seasonal flu this winter and in the past with the combination of sauerkraut and garlic. When the stomach acts like there is some disturbance, I warm up a dish of sauerkraut and add one clove of fresh raw garlic. I warm it in a pan with a little butter added.

The sauerkraut/garlic combination calms the intestines and gets rid of the bad germs and viruses. The active ingredients that kill pathogens and bad microbes are in both the sauerkraut and the raw garlic. This remedy is simple, natural and costs pennies.

## Sunshine and Supplements

Earthclinic.com has several postings about the rapidly evolving coronavirus. **Sunshine** or indoor **tanning beds** that emit ultra-violet (UV) light will help calm down an over active immune system and promote an anti-inflammatory immune responses. Real sunshine gives you real vitamin D3 sulfate, not the synthetic variation (Chlorocalciferol) you can buy in a bottle that is also used as a rodenticide.

| **Testing for Acidity and Oxygen levels** |
| --- |
| **pH Tape** - measure urine & saliva acidity/alkalinity |
| **Oximeter** - used to measure blood oxygen levels |

Normal is 94 or higher. Buy an Oximeter online. More information on this list can be found in my **Immune Restoration Handbook** available at lebeaubooks.com.

## Acid urine pH need for recovery
## An Alkaline pH is linked to a chronic infection

**Test pH-** measure your saliva and urine pH using pH tape (5.5 to 8.5). Your saliva pH should be at or above 6.4 and your urine pH should be at or below 6.4 while fighting the infection. What you don't want is urine pH that is alkaline above 7.0 and saliva pH that is acid or below 6.0. 1000 to 2000 mg **Vitamin C** and/or 1 teaspoon of **apple cider vinegar** in water taken every 2 hours will lower saliva pH and help speed recovery. See the "Immune Restoration Handbook" for a more information on how balance  your pH.

## Glutathione for Treating Pneumonia

**Cytokine Storm- Glutathione** credited with recovery from Covid-19 pneumonia by R. Horowitz, et al - Published in "Respiratory Med Case Report"

**"Purpose:** Infection with COVID-19 potentially can result in severe outcomes and death from "cytokine storm syndrome", resulting in novel coronavirus pneumonia (NCP) with severe dyspnea, acute respiratory distress syndrome (ARDS), fulminant myocarditis and multi-organ dysfunction with or without disseminated intravascular coagulation. No published treatment to date has been shown to adequately control the inflammation and respiratory symptoms associated with COVID-19, apart from oxygen therapy and assisted ventilation. We evaluated the effects of using high dose oral and/or IV glutathione in the treatment of 2 patients with dyspnea secondary to COVID-19 pneumonia."

**Methods:** A trial of 2 g of PO or IV glutathione was used in both patients and improved their dyspnea within one hour of use. Repeated use of both 2000 mg of PO and IV glutathione was effective in further relieving respiratory symptoms.

**Conclusion:** Oral and IV glutathione, glutathione precursors (**N-acetyl-cysteine**) and alpha lipoic acid may represent a novel treatment approach for blocking NFKappaB and addressing "cytokine storm syndrome" and respiratory distress.

## Lomatium Dissectum for treating Pneumonia

**Symptoms** of a chest cold or pneumonia are shortness of breath, coughing up yellow mucus or sputum, pain in a chest area or a drop in blood oxygen levels as measured with an Oximeter. The most effective treatments are Lomatium dissectum or oral drop on hydrogen peroxide in water plus following a healthy diet.

**Lomatium Dissectum.** Use as directed on the label or take 20 drops in a little water 3to 5 times a day Persons do better if they also get up and walk. Note: About 1% of people using lomatium dissectum may develop a skin rash. Discontinue and take an antihistamine like Benadryl. See a doctor for more info.

Drink water frequently and take large doses of powdered vitamin C. For product sources, check with a local health food store. Glutathione precursors also include n-acetyl cysteine, milk thistle, natural selenium, Colostrum and whey protein.

Consider trying the following for additional lung support. They include **colloidal silver** nasal inhalers, **oregano oil,** peeled **garlic toes**, **whole cloves** or a **yellow onion cut in half** placed in a cloth bag near the patient's nose. Inhale the vapors while taking a deep breath. Steam inhalation with one of the above items added will also help improve breathing.

## Diet - Important Therapeutic Foods

**Do eat Organic foods** - Non-GMO when possible.
**Do eat pickled foods** including dill pickles, pickled beets, sauerkraut, pickled cauliflower, pickled mushrooms, and other pickled vegetables. *Vinegar kills viruses,* as does lemon, lime, and sauerkraut juice; also ascorbic acid (vitamin C)
**Do drink -** Kombucha tea, also licorice root tea, rosehips tea, green tea and ginger root tea.
**Do eat organic broths** like Organic free-range chicken broth with Wakame flakes added – this increases body heat.
**Do eat homemade soups** like **potato leek soup** or chicken broth or stock with vegetables.

**Do eat small meals** and one clove of **raw garlic** 3X a day.
**Do eat raw onions and baked onions** daily.
**Cold pressed Flaxseed Oil** Eat one tablespoon of each day with organic yogurt, whey protein or mashed potatoes.
**Nutritional yeast** (Consider Kal brand) source of beta glucan
**Grassfed Whey Protein**. (source of beta glucan)
**Mushrooms - raw** - (source of beta glucan) supports immunity
**Consider a Mediterranean** or **vegetarian** diet.
**Sweeteners – xylitol, raw honey, or maple syrup**
**Grapefruit**- fresh white or red
**Raw Garlic Cloves -** olives stuffed with garlic
**Raw vegetables** plus dandelion greens
**Sauerkraut -** eat once or twice daily with a sliced clove of raw garlic. Eliminates Covid-19 from the intestines and stools.

## Whole Lemon Olive Oil remedy (for neuropathy)

This drink will benefit anyone with nerve damage, heart or kidney disease, chronic fatigue, cancer, liver damage, covid-19 and other viral infections. Drink it once day for a month and experience for yourself what it does. Drink it once or twice a week and experience its amazing benefits. Here it is:

| |
|---|
| 1/2 medium or large lemon (seeds, rind et all) or one whole small lemon. 1 cup of organic apple juice and 1 tablespoon Virgin Olive Oil 1/4 teaspoon of cayenne powder or take one cayenne capsule with the drink. |

Place all ingredients in a blender and run at high speed for one minute. Drink as is or pass through a strainer to remove partial pieces that did not blend properly. Enjoy!

## Foods to Avoid - What Not to Eat

**NO MILK OR ICE CREAM** – limit consumption to organic A2 milk, organic yogurt, kefir or sour cream or Nancy's naturally fermented cottage cheese. Avoid regular hard cheese as it promotes mucus.

**AVOID** WHITE WHEAT GRAIN PRODUCTS. NO white bread, pasta, pizza, rolls and donuts. Go easy on all grains until you recover.

**AVOID** refined white sugar products and artificial sweeteners. NO cake, cookies, donuts, etc.

**AVOID** sodas, and other drinks to which corn syrup have been added.

**Avoid Aspartame (a neurotoxin)**, Sucralose or other synthetic sweeteners.

**Avoid** beef, pork and lunchmeats until your doctor finds the intestinal and respiratory infection is gone.

**Avoid** most cold cereals – but especially any with corn or soybeans in them.

**Avoid** most processed foods including smoked foods or fried, and fast foods.

### Spiritual Help - Pray for Guidance, and have Faith

We live in a multi-dimensional universe. There is the visible and the invisible. There are opposites to everything that exists. Positive vs. negative; good vs. evil; health vs. sickness; energy vs. fatigue; happiness vs. sadness; hope vs. despair; God vs. Satan; light vs. darkness; friend vs. foe; pain vs. pleasure, predestination vs. free will, and many others. If you are in real need and are persistent, God will listen and respond to the prayers. Use your favorite prayer or consider the following that I offer here -

---

*In the name of the Father, and of the Son, and of the Holy Spirit. Blessed be Jesus, true God and true man. Look down upon your children here on earth, and protect us from all that is evil, misleading, and unjust. Keep our hopes alive, and teach us to love one another and to forgive all those whom have injured us. Teach us to not judge others, to overcome personal addictions, and help us to make worthy choices to heal our body, mind and spirit. Thank you for listening. Amen.*

---

Editor's Note: For periodical updates to this booklet on any important news on treating Covid-19, you may visit keephopealive.org or lebeaubooks.com at your convenience.

# Shopping List

- **Hydrogen Peroxide 3%** in the brown bottle or **35% food grade H2O2** with dropper pipette (SARS-Cov-2 - Antiviral)
- **Nutribiotic Grapefruit Seed extract capsules** with Echinacea and Wormwood. (Antiviral)
- **Cayenne capsules**- blocks ACE2 receptor from the Covid virus (Anti-inflammatory - dissolves blood clots)
- **Serrapeptase enzymes** - blocks ACE2 receptors from the Covid virus. (Anti-inflammatory - dissolves blood clots)
- **N-Acetyl Cysteine** - increases glutathione (anti-inflammatory)
- **Colostrum** or **Lactoferrin** - blocks ACE2 receptors from Covid virus - (Antiviral, Antibodies and Anti-inflammatory)
- **Vitamin C** powder (Buffered C-Complex) calcium ascorbate, rose hips, acerola & bioflavonoids.
- **Goldenseal Root capsules** (Antiviral) or **Berberine**
- **Thyme or Fenugreek Thyme** - (inactivates SARS-CoV-2)
- **Oregano** (Oregamax) (Antiviral)
- **Neem leaf** or Neem bark (Antiviral)
- **Lomatium Dissectum** – for pneumonia (Antiviral)
- Colloidal silver
- Flaxseed oil – cold pressed
- Tincture of Iodine
- **Zinc** gluconate or sulfate or picolinate (support immunity)
- Raw honey
- **Propolis** (Anti-viral)
- **Kelp tablets or capsules** (supports immunity)
- **Cod Liver Oil** (supports immunity)
- **pH Tape (5.5 to 8.0)** Micro Essential
- **Sauerkraut-** (anti viral- anti bacterial)
- **Nutritional yeast -**source of beta glucan - supports immunity
- **Raw garlic** (Anti-viral and supports immunity)
- **Dandelion greens** - ACE2 blocker for SARS-Cov-2
- **Local eggs from pasteurized cows**
- **Organic Non-GMO** foods and vegetables